CONFESSIONS OF A COUNTRY BOY

THOROGOOD

Published by Thorogood

10-12 Rivington Street London EC2A 3DU

Telephone: 020 7749 4748 • Fax: 020 7729 6110

Email: info@thorogood.ws

Web: www.thorogood.ws

A CIP catalogue record for this book is available
from the British Library.

ISBN 1 85418 246 3

Cover and Book designed by Driftdesign

Printed in Great Britain by Ashford Colour Press.

Published in association with the

www.acornmagazines.co.uk

Dedication

Dedicated to the many who helped me into boyhood scrapes –
and to the few who tried to get me out of them!
A special bouquet for Tubby's long-suffering Mum, whose regular
cleaning-up service saved me from even more deserved punishment.

The Spell

I don't suppose the sunshine kissed
Those buttercups with any more love
Than now can muster
Nor could a hedgerow meal have been
The sweeter for all that extra quiet
Spread round the pastures
Outdoor magic does not dim for
Horse or bird or man or tree
The spell is master

I can't believe the moonlight danced
On better crops with much more care
Than now's rotation
And did a hedge grow just to cry
The sharper for all the extra miles
Crushed round the pastures?
Outdoor magic must not dim for
Horse or bird or man or tree
The spell must master

I won't accept the sepia looks
Are bitter clues to a fonder heart
Than now can tender
We see a hedge throw one real smile
The wider for all those old friends
Lost round the pastures
Outdoor magic has to win for
Horse and bird and man and tree
Who want a master.

Keith Skipper

Contents

Broad smiles and short trousers in the playground. Keith Skipper (right) with his two elder brothers, Maurice (centre) and Malcolm, posing for a family photograph at Beeston village school in the early 1950s.

Introduction

If confession is good for the soul, I ought to be in a rare state of grace!

Sprawled across the couch of reflection, surrounded by warm voices and smiling faces impossible to ignore, I have been urged to spill the boyhood beans.

Time may have embellished one or two memories, and the odd name has been changed to protect the guilty, but these rural ramblings can be taken as a reasonably fair and accurate record of my formative years in the middle of Norfolk. Of course, I have taken full advantage of the lifting of restrictions on the Countryside Official Secrets Act (sub-section 12, Rustic Reminiscences) to reveal the truth behind certain colourful episodes. That means dear old chums Tubby, Ernie and Rodney might as well accept that they were there and did indeed play pivotal roles in some of Beeston's more outlandish moments.

I have worked overtime to be fair in apportioning any blame attached to these rich instalments of country life in the 1950s. Indeed, the discerning reader will note how regularly I am prepared to shoulder extra burdens of guilt. That is testament to the way I was brought up to take the rap when all weak excuses failed.

To family and friends on whose toes I trod in my clumsy hob-nailed boots, sincere thanks for remarkable forbearance. To all others who wondered why I tip-toed past their doors with a sheepish smile, belated apologies for a few unsolved crimes. (But it really wasn't my idea to put itching powder on the chapel seats.)

I am grateful to Pippa Bastin and her Norfolk Journal colleagues in providing a ready platform for these confessions. My wife and sons have indulged me dutifully during preparation, especially while I slipped into misty-eyed mode and took them down yesterday's leafy lanes.

For splendid pictorial backing I am particularly indebted to Ron Shaw and his Litcham Historical Society friends and the late Clifford Temple, whose friendship I valued for many years. For helping to paint pictures in words, I acknowledge the wonderful brushes of imagination first placed in my hands by Mrs Webdale and Mrs Tann at Beeston Primary School.

Distance may lend enchantment, but my country childhood has inspired much more than rampant nostalgia. I relish every chance to extol the virtues of a golden era when Norfolk life was quieter, slower, simpler... and able to take youthful misdemeanours in its stride.

Keith Skipper

Cromer, 2002

*In **January** should sun appear,*

March and April will pay full dear.

January Japes

Trail to Breadland

I still sleep better when the wind is banging on my bedroom window. It goes back to childhood and wintry blasts easy to measure by creaks and crashes from the old walnut tree. When it was in full cry beyond the well we shared with next door, and the men had come home from the fields with collars up and sombre talk of snow in the air, we knew there was a good prospect of another adventure in wonderland.

An earnest little prayer accompanied that icy symphony welling up from the orchard, walnut tree branches providing most of the percussion as we snuggled beneath extra blankets and waited for the next crescendo. It soon became apparent if that prayer had been answered as we huffed on white-crusted panes and sleeved out a view past the well, transformed overnight into an igloo with handle.

Winter Wonderland... but snow could bring hardships to country life as well.

While open comparisons with the great white-out of 1947 were scarcely encouraged, it was the inevitable yardstick for any heavy falls in the decade or so that followed. With food rationed and coal in short supply, that notorious winter just after the war stood for gloom and hardship. Youngsters tempted into hand-rubbing delight as temperatures dipped, winds freshened and snowflakes danced were given sharp reminders of country life being reduced to a grim struggle for survival.

Still, grown-ups tended to exaggerate, especially in huddles mardling about the weather, and generally failed to see the positive side of a short period of fending for yourself. Our village was in a hollow, the parish church standing sentry on one side and the old red barn keeping look-out on the other. It didn't take a meteorological genius to fathom we were likely to get bunged up for a day or two if snow came riding in either way on a puckish breeze. Part of the charm of living there, a useful little test in self-sufficiency and community care... Our youthful philosophical musings might have been tinged with regret over the need to close schools, both in the village and further afield, but some prices were worth paying if valuable lessons could be sculpted out of walls of snow.

We compensated for missing a test on long division or fractions by battling through to the doors of elderly neighbours to take orders for vital provisions from the village shop. A hastily constructed sledge transported a precarious mountain of cardboard boxes along hazardous lanes, skating on the lilypits and other important diversions put on ice until social duties had been completed. Yes, we did experience a little glow of satisfaction, and several grateful folk insisted we keep a few coppers for ourselves, but it made a wonderful change from open chastisement for breathing the same air as more mature members of the local population. Perhaps they were jealous because we could run quicker and hide better when the occasion demanded.

Our brief but glorious elevation to the status of useful members of society at a time of crisis reached epic levels when the parish ran out of bread. There was no immediate prospect of fresh supplies getting through from Litcham Bakery a couple of miles away. All regular routes were blocked. Snow-ploughs could make no inroads. Teams of men with shovels fought hopeless fights as unrelenting winds whipped up bigger drifts all around. Toast for tea was a luxury confined to a few homes where bread-making ingredients and know-how remained on the family menu.

We volunteered to haul on our Scott of the Antarctic balaclavas along with warmest clothing and deepest boots. Only the huskies were missing as we set out across virgin-white fields, guessing where ditches ought to be on a made-up trail to Breadland. Ernie made dreadful puns about using our loaf and following a star in the yeast, but we left nature to exact a measure of retribution with a spectacular avalanche shed by an oak tree while our smirking colleague stood beneath. He laughed back when we sank into holes on the edge of acres thought to have housed sugarbeet a few weeks before. A well-trodden path through packed snow came as sheer luxury. They didn't put out flags or send a band to signal our arrival in Litcham. A bad-tempered dog snapped at our tired heels and a woman scraping her doorstep asked why we hadn't better things to do with our time. We pelted the dog, ignored the woman and prepared to claim our booty.

Triumph melted into torment, elation into utter embarrassment. The bakery was deserted, and a sharp-faced man who lived two doors away informed us with not a little relish that a gang of Tittle-shall men and boys had struggled through dreadful conditions to claim the last batch just before noon. We cursed those Amundsens who had traipsed across fields from another direction to leave us no crumbs of comfort. Our role was that of defeated troops forced to go home to eat big dollops of humble pie.

A rapid thaw set in the following day. A packed baker's van resumed normal service before the end of the week. We were back at school, dreading any mention of an ill-fated trek or being given one of those infernal exercises beginning: "It takes four village lads two hours 17 minutes to walk across seven snow-covered fields..."

Good jobs to miss

When it came to New Year resolutions down on the farm, I had no trouble sorting out my top two as soon as burgeoning muscles threatened to pitch me into serious action. I worked overtime to steer clear of knockin' and toppin' sugarbeet and carting mountains of fresh muck from one fragrant spot to another.

These were winter's main dirty jobs, demanding resolution, staying power and a fundamental belief that getting close to nature meant being covered in mud and anything else that arrived in large dollops on a bleak January morning. My interest in strange rural rituals did not extend to becoming part of them while wind, frost, sleet, snow and the occasional mocking finger of sunlight chased across the landscape.

It wasn't enough to suggest I wasn't cut out for such things. Other boys took up the hook, pitchfork and squelching challenge even if they were destined for pen-pushing duties in a cosy office far from endless rows and smelly piles. And there were plenty of small, wiry characters making light of unglamorous roles as winter's calendar unfolded. Size was no barrier. It was simply a matter of attitude, settling into the right rhythm and getting on with tasks that had to be done.

My back still ached from eternities of singling behind father's flashing hoe when sugarbeet plants first blinked through the soil. At least the weather was warmer then, and sixpence a row took some of the pain away. I served a useful apprenticeship as a muck-shifter while looking after Ida Burrell's chickens on a Saturday morning. A small wheelbarrow packed with high-octane material was an affront to my sensitive nature. It did nothing to prepare me for an Everest of steaming manure stacked precariously on a wheezing tumbril, asking for redistribution at the bottom of the ten-acre meadow.

Whenever I was reminded that certain answers laid in the soil (and associated substances), I pointed out politely but emphatically that I had no interest in even listening to the questions. Any traces of guilt over lack of proper contact with the sugarbeet harvest, from banging together two specimens from a large root crop to shift clinging mould to heaving them, defoliated and fairly clean, on to another lorry bound for the factory, tended to disappear as mud thickened and cold gnawed at a straggling army along the Norfolk trenches.

Even now I use knockin' and toppin' and spreading fresh muck as perfect antidotes for too much gilding of the 1950s lily. Romantic notions about farming's 'good old days' can be kept in reasonable check with vivid descriptions of onerous chores before the cavalry of mechanisation charged over churned-up headlands. And I don't think you had to experience those chores on any kind of regular basis to offer heartfelt thanks they no longer clutter the land.

Humour is another useful weapon with which to honestly till yesterday's furrows, and two of my favourite Norfolk yarns feature the very subjects under discussion. I read nothing significant into that, although it has been suggested by friends of psychological leaning that it could betray lingering paranoia over abject failure to meet certain expectations in my youth...

A couple of farm-workers were busy on the barn roof when time arrived for their midday break. "Cum yew on, Horry, less go down arter our grub. Reckon I're got spam agin now thass Tewsday... blarst me, bor, we're stuck up here! Sum sorft fewl he' knocked the ladder away. What are we gorn ter dew?"

Muckspreading – one of winter's main dirty jobs in the 'good old days' before mechanisation charged over the headlands

"I know", said Horry. "There's a nice fresh pile o'muck down there. I'll jump down an' tell yew how deep that is." He took the plunge. "How deep is it?" called Fred. "That only cum up ter yer ankles."

"Right" said Fred, "I'm a'cumin' ter join yew." He leapt from the barn roof – and was covered in fresh muck from head to foot.

"Yew duzzy ole tewl! Thowt yew said it only cum up ter yer ankles", he spluttered.

"Ah" explained Horry, "I fergot ter tell yew I went in head fust!"

The other story concerns two labourers pulling sugarbeet on a large, open field in cutting wind and icy rain on a Monday morning in January during the early days of the Second World War. One of them had happened to scan a newspaper before coming to work. He said to his partner: "I see in the EDP them ole Jarmans hev gone inter Warsaw."

When they reached the end of the row about 30 minutes later, the other tugged at his coat collar, brushed mud from sacking round his waist and squeezed water from the peak of his cap as he gazed up at brooding skies.

"Well," he remarked drily, "They hent got much o'a day for it."

They resumed knockin' and toppin' without another word.

The generation game

While strait-laced days of being seen but not heard might have been numbered, a Norfolk country child of the 1950s still had to tread with extreme caution through dull weeks after all those heady festive delights.

Tied to the old homestead by long, dark evenings, unfriendly weather and a basic belief that growing lads and the world about them were much safer for a teatime curfew, I viewed January's restrictions with some trepidation.

Renewed zeal for homework wore off about five minutes into the first algebra jungle of the New Year. Sadly, my mathematical machete remained blunt for the rest of my career. The History of Mr Polly lost some of its appeal when no-one else in the room showed the slightest interest in a radical theory about early-20th century drop-outs. Blow-football matches were abandoned when Dad commandeered the table for peeling potatoes – such an ignominious pitch invasion when you were leading 6-0 – and Radio Luxembourg came and went even more regularly than hopes of an early Spring.

For all the frustrations and constraints placed on a busy cottage scene by a large family in limited space, it did no good to complain. Retribution was swift and terminal if anyone was daft enough to mutter: "Cor, I ent half bored." Up Wooden Hill to Blanket Fair with a smart ding of the lug as substitute for a bedtime beverage.

Such brands of instant justice may not be too fashionable in these more 'enlightened' times, but I bridle instantly when my sons or their compatriots suggest there's a distinct lack of incentive to find something useful to do. I have been known to add sharp riders after a few seconds on my old-fashioned high horse, pointing out how we had to make our own fun from the flimsiest of material and opportunity while today's pampered crew are spoilt for choice but too lazy to see it.

Ah, the old generation game! What a source of useful social headlines through the ages, with countless chastised children growing up to become echoes of parents they had ached to defy, ignore or contradict. I knew how far not to go after a few early nights, but decided to exorcise some of the anguish by carrying out what could well have been the village's first lifestyle opinion poll.

I asked a hand-picked selection of folk, the majority linked to the land all their working lives, if they had ever been bored as youngsters... or found current tasks tedious and monotonous. A couple of chaps busy on a cheerless sugarbeet scene said their schooldays had been boring, but they could not recommend knockin' and toppin' as the most satisfying form of employment. An old ploughman – well, he seemed ancient to me as he mentioned hard furrows after the First World War – claimed he'd never had time to be bored. "But I dew wish I'd dun a bit more book-larnin'. Thass the cummin' thing" he prophesied.

Our local lengthman, responsible for keeping roads tidy, ditches clear and verges trimmed, would not exchange fresh air and freedom for a better-paid job cooped up in an office. Yes, he had been fed-up at times as a youngster, mainly through a lack of sporting interests, but he saw no need for anyone to feel deprived of anything in the countryside: "We're much more our own masters than that lot in the towns and cities" he smiled.

Perhaps some of my interviewees were being rather kind to themselves and their community. One or two clearly aimed to humour me, probably after warnings from Dad that I was on the loose with notebook and joined-up writing. Even so, there was no call to feed all the information into a computer to confirm what I knew already; the older generation loved to hand down valuable advice, and this invariably included guarding against boredom and lack of ambition by making more of education than they had managed themselves. Generally, for all their personal misgivings and shortcomings, and those spiteful January winds whipping across the headlands, they still found more rewards than regrets in roles they had been allotted.

Of course, I didn't know how soon this vast rural army would be decimated by the march of mechanisation and drastic changes in farming practices. As Adrian Bell, doyen of East Anglian country-side writers, put it so adroitly in one of his 1970s essays reflecting on old agricultural ways: "Only now do I realise the riches that must have leaked through the sieve of my attention."

My little exercise did achieve one important breakthrough. It helped alleviate the risk of rampant boredom on at least one January journey over 40 years ago. The bonus was to be invited to introduce the topic of town v country living in the grammar school classroom.

One boy had the temerity to yawn when I presented the case for rural supremacy with all the passion I could muster. I think he was asleep as hands went up to tell me I had a fair way to go before claiming a podium in the debating society.

Hard graft on the January farming scene. For all the rigours of back-bending jobs, most workers found more rewards than regrets in the Norfolk roles they had been allotted in the 1950s.

*If it rains in **February** every day,*

In June you're sure of plenty of hay.

February Frolics

That flippin' pancake...

We meandered rather than maraudered, a small clutch of country youngsters with enough patience to wait for mischief to present itself. Or perhaps we just had a lazy streak.

Living in a small village soaked in agricultural ways had significant shortcomings. There were but a few means of earning pocket money, with washing eggs, feeding pigs and digging gardens the mainstays. Not a lot of laughs if you were allergic to getting your hands dirty and didn't like pigs.

Rounding up the usual suspects was a formality when it came to identifying perpetrators of heinous pranks like jamming the privy door against all comers, however desperate, or popping frogspawn into school inkwells, making sure enough targets would be visited by females of tender sensibilities.

Being singled out as a 'bright boy' was no insurance against selection for classroom detention or an early departure up Wooden Hill to Blanket Fair. Indeed, it could be a massive disadvantage when a particularly clever ruse was being investigated. "Must have been you thought of that!" brought a blush of confirmation and the obligatory swift punishment.

Most of my best ideas surfaced well away from the old homestead, especially after that traumatic Shrove Tuesday when my culinary urges got completely out of hand. I appointed myself king of the kitchen on arriving home from school to discover Mother and her bike were elsewhere.

Two younger sisters found me an apron, a mixing bowl and all ingredients deemed necessary for making pancakes. They dragged out the frying pan, showed me how to light the oil stove and stood back in wonder as eggs, flour and milk scattered in all directions. My creative juices flowed as sizzling noises intensified.

I had never been beyond fried onions before, and that had come under Dad's Sunday morning supervision. This was a giant leap into the unknown. No recipe book for guidance, and if one or two finer points of domestic etiquette were being overlooked, well, two impressed sisters showed no intention of telling tales.

They licked their lips as I licked my fingers and the big metal spoon now being transformed into a wizard's wand. Spellbound at my own newfound audacity, I called for sugar and treacle to anoint my very first golden brown creation. More thick, creamy mixture slid easily into the pan while my sampling audience heralded an unexpected Tuesday triumph, albeit with just a dash too much fried onion seasoning.

It was here that any remnants of reason were washed away on a tide of bravado. I simply flipped as my second pancake demanded a traditional celebration. Urged on by siblings doing a passable impression of the crowd at our Coronation Day sports sack race on Lew Dack's meadow, I launched my tasty delight towards the whitewashed ceiling.

Like an animated professor wielding a butterfly net, I broke the bounty's fall with a perfectly-timed stretch. It smacked obligingly against the bottom of the pan. I tossed again with a triumphant whoop. What a doddle! What a debut! What outrageous fun! Mrs Beeton, eat your heart out!

I didn't know much about the laws of gravity, but I knew that the pancake ought to have re-entered part of the stratosphere round the kitchen table within a few seconds. The girls gaped upwards as if waiting for a divine explanation. I stood with my empty pan, perplexed, alone, awkward, confused and suddenly aware how rousing kitchen capers can fall so flat. Two discoveries restored dramatic life to this Shrove Tuesday tableau.

"It's stuck to the lightshade!" I cried.

"Here comes Mum!" they yelled.

"Cut her off at the gate!" I implored.

One sister chased down the yard to employ well-rehearsed delaying tactics – "Oh, I've got something to show you in the shed, Mum" – while the other helped me break the Mid-Norfolk indoor record for erasing evidence of an impromptu cooking session carried out by a novice in fading light on a February afternoon.

Well, most of the evidence. We couldn't reach the errant pancake, and so had to prepare for the longest teatime in Norfolk family history. Would the deadly lightshade give up its slithering secret while we were all seated at the table?

The suspense was dreadful and I developed a stiff neck stealing furtive glances above. Mother's pancakes lacked their usual appeal. After what appeared to be the decisive shift towards dropping in Dad's direction, I pointed to the offending object and blurted out a full confession.

As I sobbed myself to early sleep, vowing not to get caught smoking on Ash Wednesday, a little consoling thought crossed my mind.

At least my pancake-making had a light touch.

Slow on the drawl

It was my turn to be James Stewart, a part more worthy of my talents despite a vociferous playground lobby to saddle me with Gabby Hayes. Apparently, I acted quite old for my age.

I didn't mind a stint as George Formby, although it had to be one of the few impressions where the Lancashire comedian got by with a broad Norfolk accent and without a ukulele. My toothy grin and bold experiments with Brylcream were strong compensating factors.

A week as Humphrey Bogart ended in some disarray over the length of my raincoat – it hardly covered my weather-lashed knees – the angle of my hat, and the lack of a convincing world-weary look. I had worked hard on the mannerisms and voice, but when I called a girl my shweetheart behind the bikeshed, she landed me a shtinging shidewinder and told me not to be so shtupid.

So the James Stewart role came as a timely relief. We had so much in common. It took a lot to get us riled. We betrayed a single-minded integrity that had to become the envy of friend and foe alike. He was stationed in Norfolk during the war. I arrived towards the end of hostilities to take over the runway watch when he went home.

I can still break into a respectful impression of that wonderful delivery, sort of shy but sincere, emotional but never weak, slow on the drawl but quick on the draw as he galloped on to our aerodrome in cowboy gear to inspire countless playtime repeats from Where The River Bends, The Man From Laramie and Broken Arrow.

We had to make much of our own entertainment in those days before television took a hold on family life. The man came round with moving pictures on a Friday night, setting his projector whirring and our imaginations spinning in the Nissen hut that was our village hall. There were variations in our diet during the early 1950s. We shared a good chuckle with the likes of Abbott and Costello, Laurel and Hardy, Red Skelton, The Three Stooges, The Little Rascals, Norman Wisdom, the real George Formby, Old Mother Riley and Tarzan.

Even so, only the cowboys could ensure an orderly retreat across the old aerodrome concrete paths as we hit the darkness. A smart slap on the thigh (your own) and a whispered "giddyup!" signalled the youthful posse's instant acceptance of law enforcement. Straight home and no mucking about.

If James Stewart was my king of the corral, Hopalong Cassidy had to be crown prince of the prairies. William Boyd rode through no less than 66 films as the gentleman cowboy who wore black, many of them with dear old Gabby Hayes in tow. Walter Gabriel in a stetson, Gabby provided the comic relief all good Westerns needed. And he had a thing about baked beans...

We also lapped up those every-expense-spared serials, each instalment ending with our hero teetering on the edge of destruction. (A bit like Ernie, Tubby and me tackling another round of country dancing in the school playground).

"Be sure not to miss the next thrilling instalment on show in this theatre... ". Our old Nissen hut, a theatre! As big a laugh as pretending not to know if he would escape from that old mine before the dynamite went off.

There were also big dollops of romance and sentiment to confront. I brushed aside several tears with a crumpled crisp packet when it became obvious that gorgeous Ava Gardner was more interested in smarmy old Howard Keel than a Beeston boy with weather-lashed knees. The worst was over by the time the Showboat had gone round the bend.

Ernie spotted Marilyn Monroe's pouting potential at an early stage of her career. Tubby brought unexpected maturity to the Friday night cinema debating society three rows back with serious references to the acting abilities of Joyce Grenfell and Margaret Rutherford. We knew he hadn't flipped completely as he sized up Ginger Roger's legs, Virginia Mayo's hair-do and Jane Russell's beautiful pair of eyes.

We graduated from Beeston's palace of varieties to Dereham's Exchange Cinema on school outings to see the Coronation and the ascent of Everest. Wonderful occasions, but we had to go back to the Nissen hut for Pathe News highlights of the Stanley Matthews Cup Final in 1953. Later that summer, England's cricketers won back the Ashes – with Norfolk's own Bill Edrich at the crease – and James Stewart stumped another screenful of baddies. A truly golden year. I even pushed Ava Gardner to one side for a few minutes.

James Stewart came back to Norfolk to reflect on wartime exploits before he rode off into the sunset. When the lights go down so it can be yesterday again, I steal an affectionate glance at the Nissen hut on the aerodrome where Friday night adventures were simply the best.

James Stewart
My king of the corral

A bleach of the priest

One of the beauties of spending your entire growing-up time in one small place is a warmth of familiarity ready to spread itself over every recollection, every homecoming. Even though my old village may have undergone many changes since I cut the umbilical binder-twine that held me fast for over 18 years, there remain plenty of physical mementoes to go with the emotional pull. And, delight-fully, one or two mysteries linger on as well.

I was a curious lad. By that, I mean inquisitive, eager to know a bit more than was good for me, perhaps something on the juicy side to dish out to open-mouthed classmates in the playground. It could send your stock rising, your lane credibility soaring, if you had a slice of scandal to share the morning after the fight before. They all knew something had happened outside the pub at closing time. The police were summoned. PC Cordy came as quick as he could from Litcham on his bike. Did he make any arrests? What was the cause of this uprising? Were 'outsiders' behind it all? I could weave a three-act drama of epic proportions out of such questions, finding key roles for Scotland Yard, Swaffham Mafia, Dereham CID and the British Boxing Board of Control as imagination ran riot. This art came in very handy later on when I had to create fresh excuses for failing to hand in homework or explain why my new long trousers saw fit to dispense with any material around the right knee area. I was far ahead of my time when it came to fashion on the rural catwalk.

Powers of invention – or, as I preferred to call it, a healthy creative streak – made me an automatic choice as leader of the parish inves-tigation department, junior branch. Early jobs included trying to discover what the Misses Squires kept in the other biscuit tin behind the curtain where they disappeared to find little rewards for errands. The one with George V on the lid held treacle toffees, and was opened regularly to helpful children. The one bearing a steam train, a true monarch of the rails, stayed sealed, mysterious, out of reach. Maybe it was empty, a forlorn ornament from a previous domestic scene, but I was determined to transform it into Pandora's Box.

It contained everything from rare cigarette cards to gold sovereigns, treasure maps to letters from the First World War trenches, as I was spattered with inquiries after every call at the ancient sisters' homestead. The fact I changed the contents so often did little to diminish the impact of my uncanny probing qualities on a receptive playground community. Similar rapt attention greeted revelations about a dastardly gang who had pilfered lead off the parish church roof, swinging Tarzan-like through the midnight blackness from tree to tower, and feather-brained bantam rustlers, trapped in a coop by yelping dogs and backsides too big for the job. Neither incident made the newspapers, but my admirers knew a proper sleuth when they heard one.

Even so, one mystery fell beyond even my remarkable range of investigative methods. It had long been put round the village in very loud whispers that our parson took a cold bath every morning. Quite why this titbit of gossip should so arouse general interest, especially among the young, never became fully evident, although I suspect a general air of intrigue hanging round the old rectory fed fanciful notions. It was easily the most imposing building in our little world, smothered in foliage and history. Formerly surrounded by a moat, the house was burned down in the reign of James I and rebuilt on the same site. Three storeys high but still able to hide itself among trees away from the heart of the village and the church, it represented an elegance and status well beyond the majority of locals.

I was volunteered to get as close as possible to the building and its inhabitant to find out if this story about his ablutions was based on facts. Only later did it dawn on me that for some it was a useful exercise in trying to land a bright but foolhardy lad in hot water. While I was occupied at one end of the parish, there might be a chance of peace and order breaking out at the other.

I could scarcely wander up to his front door and claim to be a sanitation inspector checking on clerical washing habits. I didn't have the equipment to pass as a plumber or window cleaner and everyone knew I couldn't stand heights. He was Church. I was Chapel. The ecumenical ladder did not go beyond an occasional get-together to celebrate harvest or Christmas. Still, I worked alone on cases like this, issuing my own statements at the end of another painstaking inquiry...

"I crawled on my belly across the meadows from the council houses to trees and shrubs at the back of the rectory. I peered into all windows on the ground floor and head gurgling noises from a small room next to the pantry. A stirring male voice rang out with lines from a hymn about 'washing sins away', but I couldn't tell from the pitch if it was hot, cold or lukewarm water responsible for such a whitening operation. I was about to look for a way in when... "

Glorious fiction to keep me on top of the detective pile. There could be no danger of anyone contradicting my version of events or asking to keep me company on a return visit. It's easy to come clean now when I go anywhere near the grand old rectory – but the real mystery is why they didn't put me away for causing a bleach of the priest!

The **old rectory** where, it was claimed, the parson took a cold bath every morning. Keith Skipper investigated.

North Milestones

March winds and
April showers

Bring forth May flowers.

March Milestones

Canary crusade

Civilisation as we had come to know and adore it perished just before teatime on Wednesday, March 18th, 1959.

It was a week after my 15th birthday when news from the Midlands broke through to wash away Norfolk banks of pride and passion built on epic sporting feats.

Norwich City's footballers were bidding to become the first Division Three side to reach the FA Cup final. They had toppled Manchester United, Cardiff, Tottenham and Sheffield United on their way to the last four.

The first semi-final meeting with Luton at White Hart Lane, Tottenham's ground, ended in a 1-1 draw in front of a 63,500 crowd.

The Norwich City FA Cup heroes of 1958-59 who went so close to becoming the first Division Three club to reach Wembley.

Back row (left to right): Roy McCroham, Bryan Thurlow, Ken Nethercott, Barry Butler, Ron Ashman, Matt Crowe.

Front row (left to right): Errol Crossan, Terry Allcock, Terry Bly, Jimmy Hill, Bobby Brennan.

Nethercott dislocated his shoulder in the first sixth-round meeting with Sheffield United, and his place in goal was taken by Sandy Kennon for the replay and the two games against Luton.

On to the replay at St Andrew's in Birmingham with a gate of nearly 50,000 looking on and a Wembley ticket the glittering prize. It was the end of the great Canary crusade.

Little Billy Bingham scored the decisive goal after 56 minutes. One of the most thrilling runs in the history of the competition was over. All our capital plans lay in ruins. I could scarcely see the road ahead on my bike journey home from school as tears welled up and splashed all over the handlebars.

We listened to part of the wireless commentary in the grammar school's reading room at Swaffham. By the time I caught my train to Fransham and disembarked for what I hoped would be a triumphant pedal towards those famous twin towers of Wembley, the yellow and green tide had been turned back at last.

Norfolk had been taken over by football fever since early January when the Canaries defied all odds and toppled mighty Manchester United 3-0 at snowbound Carrow Road in the third round. Victory over the Busby Babes was the beginning of the big time.

As more sensational results followed, ticket queues snaked for miles and stories of hardship and sacrifice multiplied when hire-purchase agreements came under serious strain. This sort of success carried a high price.

We country lads decided to play a waiting game while men who hadn't set a foot outside the county since the war headed for the likes of Sheffield, London and Birmingham. A tinge of envy, perhaps, as they returned singing, cheering, swaying, drunk on success, but we could hang on for the headiest brew of all.

First official meeting of the Beeston Boys' Branch of the Norwich-for-Wembley Club was not very well attended. Both of us swore allegiance to the cause as rats scuttled among straw bales at the back of the barn. We agreed to invite lads from the neighbouring villages of Litcham and Mileham to our next gathering.

That did the trick. We were warned such rustic benevolence could spark a return to hostilities along the lines of the 1956 Test Match Wars. Our second official meeting brought a much more healthy attendance of four and a clause in the constitution that all members should be completely home-grown and likely to be resident in the parish until schooldays were done.

Conviction grew. The Canaries were poised to make football history. We had to save enough cash to get to Wembley to cheer them on to the ultimate prize. That meant our skiffle group, The Swede-bashers, being pegged back in the race for fame and fortune when the guitar fund was disbanded.

I asked for "This decision took real pluck" to be recorded in the minutes. Fortunately, my request was drowned out by a fervent rendition of "On The Ball, City!" the anthem rapidly becoming as famous as 'The Blaydon Races' and a perfect weapon with which to frighten rats at the back of the barn.

Birthday money boosted the kitty. Important questions about travelling arrangements were raised. Was it too far to bike? Would there be a bus from the village? What about a special train stopping at Fransham? Why did Ernie think we ought to go there via a place called Soho?

Tubby asked about tickets, but we voted to leave that in abeyance until the Canaries had made it. Details would be in the paper, and surely the genuine supporters would get priority.

Then, on that Wednesday afternoon in March, 1959, a slightly-built Irishman scored a goal destined to break Norfolk hearts and draw sighs of regret from all who wanted this sporting fairytale to have a happy ending.

There were consolations to come. Luton lost in the final. The Canaries were promoted to Division Two the following year. Over a decade later, as a fully-fledged sports reporter on the local press, I covered City's elevation to Division One for the first time and their visits to Wembley for League Cup finals against Spurs and Aston Villa.

I was a member of the Radio Norfolk commentary team in 1985 when the Canaries finally tasted Wembley glory, beating Sunderland 1-0 in the Milk Cup final. But none of these exploits could possibly match the torrent of emotions unleashed by The Run of 1958-59.

We shared out the nest-egg – nearly five bob each – sniffled and choked our way through the opening lines of the Canary anthem and threw balls of bindertwine at rats still scuttling at the back of the barn.

Then we waited for the men to come home from Birmingham like soldiers from a glorious distant war.

The birthday boy

A birthday in March brought a measure of celebratory relief from the long famine between Christmas delights and our annual Sunday School bus trip to the seaside. It also meant severe tests of playground friendships after a call at the village shop just over the road clutching precious coupons from a ration book.

A few ounces of favourite sweets dominated my special occasion, although selection could be influenced by whatever was flavour of the month among my chums. Liquorice whirls, winter mixture and anything coated in coconut tended to attract hordes of admirers. Pear drops, aniseed balls and pineapple chunks left me with slightly more scope to scoff alone once Tubby and Ernie had completed their war dances of expectation.

Packets of sweet cigarettes were regular purchases before and after lessons throughout the year, not so much for the chance to imitate a cool grown-up as to complete a collection of footballers ahead of the rest of your classroom rivals. I recall spending all my birthday money – two shiny shillings – in one vain effort to unearth Number 33, a Scottish goalkeeper, as the final card in my playing pack. Tubby, who wanted Number 18 to win the race, held two spare pictures of that curly-haired custodian from north of the border, but kept them under wraps until a lap of triumph beckoned. Despite bitter disappointment, and threats to ban him from future competitions, I knew I would have been no more magnanimous given his position in such a tense shoot-out.

Ted and Violet Margarson kept our village stores, contrasting figures on our childhood canvas. Ted loved a bit of fun at the customer's expense, his banter and bonhomie echoed so appealingly in the television show Open All Hours. Similarities with the ebullient Arkwright don't end there. Ted's full moustache, ample frame, brown overall and ready humour could well have been the prototype for a corner-shop wag destined to find fame.

Mrs Margarson chided her husband quietly as he took liberties over the counter. She was gentle, patient with customers of all ages who couldn't quite make up their minds and always ready to listen as parish adventures unfolded. We confided in her often after school, telling her things we knew she wouldn't pass on to our parents. The soul of discretion in a cross-over apron.

Ted 'shopped' me for unseemly behaviour very early in my education when I went on safari in the girls' playground after asking to be excused. Inclines towards the drain sent out an obvious invitation. Ted happened to be looking across while I was in full flow, and he phoned headteacher Mrs Tann to report one of her new little boys was in danger of giving the village a bad name. It was a fair cop, and we often chuckled about this episode when Ted felt I had matured sufficiently to help him in the shop and on his delivery rounds.

An ARP warden during the war, Ted told colourful tales about the local Home Guard and a strange preoccupation with mild beer before and after vital manoeuvres. He recalled how a certain parish council election had been spiced up by a dramatic rash of colourful posters in favour of Elijah Dickerson, a kindly soul who looked after the war memorial but the most unlikely of candidates for council duties.

Ted operated at the heart of village life, taking part in concerts at the school before the war and playing a key role in Beeston's victory celebrations of June 8, 1946. He showed me the souvenir programme of events before delivering another pound of sausages. I realise now how he planted little seeds destined to blossom into my passion for local history.

E.DOWNS.
GROCER & DRAPER

E. DOWNS Licensed Tobacconist

Miss Downs poses in front of the Beeston village shop she ran in the early 1900s.

This later picture shows Ted and Violet Margarson chatting to Gordon Carter, head of the Litcham bus company. Gordon had just arrived in his shooting-brake to deliver hot midday meals to the school over the road. Both shop and school are still flourishing.

Happily, the shop continues to flourish. I dropped in recently to buy a bag of sweets for old time's sake, and was pleased to learn rationing had ended. Only minutes before I'd behaved impeccably in the school playground on being invited to officially open £130,000 worth of new facilities – including the first indoor toilets in the building's 120-year history. With my old mate Tubby on hand to prompt extra memories, I lifted the lid on a few of our less scurrilous escapades from the early 1950s.

Tubby lived almost next door to the school, and so could get to the shop quicker than the rest of our gang if a new batch of sweet cigarettes came in. Perhaps this gave him a decisive edge in any race to complete a set of footballers. As we looked at computers where inkwells used to be, and wondered if today's youngsters really enjoyed as much fun as our post-war generation, he gave me a nudge and an offer I found it impossible to refuse: "Swap you a 33 for an 18 and a gobstopper!"

Mrs Tann would have appreciated efforts to share little pleasures. Ted and Violet Margarson would have been thankful for extra trade and a cheerful conclusion to another little village adventure.

A nice cup of tea

The kettle was never far from the hob in our old homestead. Teapot and strainer worked overtime, not just in the name of family refreshment but also to welcome and sustain a constant cavalcade of visitors, expected or otherwise. It was extremely rare for any caller to leave without sampling the cup that cheers, although Father did his best to put off a certain harridan in the village notorious for her idle gossip and busy imagination. Warnings that she was on the way invariably saw him grab an old enamel bowl, turn up his trousers, peel off his socks and devote all available hot water to a feet-washing exercise.

On one memorable occasion, Mrs Tittle-Tattle was beaten to our door by the parson on his monthly circuit. He drew all kinds of biblical connotations from Father's homely ablutions, waited steadfastly for his cup of tea – and departed immediately the dear lady darkened the threshold. He couldn't stand her either. Mother mumbled something about rats, sinking ships, smelly socks and sins finding people out...

I must emphasise that this beggar-thy-neighbour game was played wholly out of respect for rules held dear by most small communities in rural Norfolk when I was a lad. Busybodies had to be kept in check, and if they couldn't take a hint, usually trimmed with harmless humour, well, a dash or two of native cunning could be employed. It wasn't out of the question for members of your own family to be given the treatment, although there were obvious dangers of revenge spirit overflowing at christenings, weddings and funerals when something a bit stronger than tea was on hand.

My earliest memories include playful jabs aimed at grown-up legs while I built brick mountains and then demolished them under the kitchen table. Gradually I matched legs and voices before kindly delivery-men crouched to chuck me under the chin and ask if I'd been a good little boy since last week. My responses must have been fairly encouraging in view of a general invitation to emerge from under the table for a few lessons in mardling and mixing before starting school. What social graces I betrayed by the time I was five owed much to the cheerful chaps who brought our groceries, bread, meat, fish, Corona, coal, newspapers, letters, freshly-charged accumulators and other necessities of domestic life.

Gordon Bailey, calling from his family store at next-door Litcham, and Reggie Burleigh, representing the Kingston & Hurn emporium in faraway Dereham, were my main mentors as their loaded vans pulled up with foodstuffs and enough avuncularity to spread over seven days. Both heeded pleas for fresh cardboard boxes to furnish my own little shop up the corner, and Reggie presented the most colourful necktie from his large collection to help me look the part behind the counter. They made sultanas and raisins disappear, drew instant pictures of cats with outrageous whiskers on pounds of lard and threatened playfully to tip grains of rice over my head so I could get married. Amusing yarns flowed around the Wednesday morning teacups, and I felt so proud to be part of these cordial gatherings. Even when I gave up shopkeeping for Test cricket in the orchard, Gordon and Reggie, the Morecambe and Wise of the groceries world, still found time to hurl greetings and jokes over the hedge. I couldn't bowl straight for chuckling. Well, at least I had a useful excuse for wayward deliveries.

Ray Hooks became another firm family favourite from Litcham. He came round with freshly-baked bread, and occasionally crumbled in the face of desperate requests for a ride in his delicious-smelling van. We sandwiched ourselves between golden loaves for an expedition up a rutted drift to the farm on the other side of the universe. The fact we did it, adored it and got back well in time for dinner stands as a glowing tribute to the community spirit and trust that welded us together on the village rounds about half a century ago. Today's health-and-safety troops would suffer apoplexy at the very thought of such antics, while a blatant lack of counselling after our bread-run adventures suggests we were lucky to survive the Dark Ages of Rural Degradation.

Of course, regular callers in countryside areas more remote than ours served as impromptu social workers, delivering messages, medicines, gossip and geniality as well as providing a valuable listening ear and keeping a friendly eye on older customers long established as firm friends. Perhaps loneliness and illness were stronger causes for concern than fear of rural crime in those days, but with suspicious behaviour swiftly reported to police then much closer to their communities, any upset nerves could soon be soothed.

In saluting all those convivial characters on their country beats, several of them measuring unbroken service in a matter of decades, I must find a special place for the medical marvels who brought comfort and joy to households such as ours. A brood of ten, five boys and five girls, bore ample testimony to the skills of the travelling nurse at home confinements.

A vital part of the Norfolk delivery business – and our inspired family motto came out every time the kettle boiled: "Don't take any chances – send for the midwife!"

Village butcher, William Wyett (Keith Skipper's great uncle), on his rounds from Beeston with pony and trap.

April with his hack and his bill,
Plants a flower on every hill.

April Adventures

Monkey business

We didn't need the glorious excuse of legitimate antics on the first day of April to prove we could play the fool. It came quite naturally any time of the year, and we were always out to top the previous prank with an extra dash of devilment. Just occasionally, as the mercury of ambition bubbled perilously close to the top of the thermometer in our adventure pack, we came slightly unstuck. Take the monkey-on-a-rope saga when primeval screams tore the beauty out of a sun-kissed April morning.

The house beyond the orchard wall was trapped in a jungle of brambles, bushes and nettles, many of them rioting against boarded windows and locked doors. It was forbidden country, rendering a visit totally out of the question and therefore wholly desirable. A deliberately-struck cricket ball deep into the under-growth proved a perfect passport. We edged towards a small window from which the nailed wood had been removed, peeped inside and sniffed the musty blackness.

Gripped with an uncommon bout of politeness – "No, after you!" – we toyed with the idea of a complete tactical withdrawal until an official invitation to view had been received. But fear of other boys discovering we had come so close to entry and then skulked away drove us on into the unknown. I went in last simply because my regular role as chief look-out had assumed even greater significance since a tractor had been heard spluttering into life about six fields away. Someone had to ensure the coast was really clear.

By the time I joined Tubby and Ernie in what turned out to be a small pantry, their torchlight dancing on dusty crockery, jars with little home-made labels and empty shelves covered in old newspaper, brittle nerves had given way to cheerful bravado. We were in and a thorough inspection must follow. After shuffling past a silent grand-father clock and a Picture Post magazine opened at a spread on tombs in Egypt, I lost the vote over whether we ought to take our inquiries upstairs. I followed because it was no fun on your own thinking about Egyptian tombs downstairs. The landing creaked. A bedroom door, ajar and cobwebbed, was the next test in this eerie examination of inquisitive boyhood. Thank goodness we were too young to have been subjected to the raw delights of Hammer Films.

Suddenly my colleagues forgot all enmities that ever existed between them and clung to each other unashamedly. I tried to get rid of a shriek and to hold on to my dinner at the same time. There, leaning against a pillow yellow with damp, staring at us with bright beady eyes, was a black monkey in a glass case. It looked as if it had just been startled from sleep. We were too scared to run.

After an eternity of shudders and shakes, we agreed the animal posed no immediate danger as it was dead and stuffed. In a moment of remarkable clarity considering our mental and physical states,

Tubby suggested we move it to a place of greater safety – our new hide-out at the top of the old barn. That broke the spell. The start of our very own zoo! It would be good company for the mice, spiders, cats and girls we planned to lure into our den.

Departure from the house of dark secrets was much quicker than the entrance. We threw a sack over our bounty, raced up the wobbly steps to gang headquarters and released the monkey from its prison. Ernie, very good at tying things, fixed it to a sort of pulley contraption he had make earlier out of an old rope found among the rusty chaff-cutters and hurdles below.

Then he showed supreme ingenuity in demonstrating how the monkey could slide down the rope at a rate of knots when the door was opened at the foot of the stairs. All we needed now was a guinea pig.

The boy who tried to catch us out on April Fools Day with a message that the most desirable girl in the school wanted to see us individually behind the gramophone after country dancing was selected for the honour. He was a bit younger than us and scarcely known for fortitude in the face of adversity. A tell-tale into the bargain, he surely deserved everything coming his way.

Well, our biology lessons had yet to feature 'heart attack', 'nervous breakdown' or 'gibbering wreck', but we received a crash course in these and a few more as he was introduced to our new-found friend. The little primate just wanted to say "Hi, mate!" but the meeting lasted no longer than it took for our victim to screech, sob and turn apoplectically white. He seemed on the verge of passing out when Ernie suggested it was only a bit of fun. That roused him into another screaming fit as he disappeared through the hedge.

The boy went home with a story no-one believed. We took the monkey back to its murky bedroom, dismantled the pulley contraption and pledged to show more passion for country dancing.

Six of the best... country lads waiting to come off the fence for another round of mischief.

The unknown soldier

Despite occasional reminders from swanky relations that we lived in 'darkest Norfolk', there was no shortage of amiable missionaries to bring us enlightening news from the big world beyond. A procession of tradesmen delivered all the latest gossip, trooping up the path like benevolent uncles to remind us what day it was.

There were Sunday treats from an ice-cream vendor with a straw hat, a bike and a box brimming with inducements to be better behaved for at least five minutes. The Thursday accumulator man did magic at the back of the wireless so Dick Barton, Mrs Dale and Archie Andrews wouldn't keep disappearing. The Saturday dinnertime Indian with tall turban and wide smile carried a bulging case and a delightful line in patter designed to soften hearts of the most reluctant Norfolk customers.

"Daddy very much like new tie!" Out slithered a silk concoction with a nearly-nude lady cavorting round the empty plates across our kitchen table. Mum called it disgraceful. Dad thought it slightly daring for Chapel services. The salesman searched in vain for more sober fare. He promised to work on his Norfolk accent before the next visit. "Daddy very good at talking squit!"

Regular callers became friends of the family, and that certainly helped take some of the sting out of parting with hard-earned money. Any new face demanded close inspection, gentle inquisition over a cup of tea wherever possible and probing discussion round the village for a few days after. Strangers were not allowed to take anyone or anything for granted – and this was long before Neighbourhood Watch schemes became an automatic part of country life. 'Darkest Norfolk' had a candle in every window.

It was most unusual to pass anyone you didn't know on the way to school, shop, Chapel, pub, village hall or even the railway station a few miles away. Fresh passengers on the green bus picking up its human cargo around the parish for a day out in town or city were vetted most carefully. The driver was on first-name terms by the time of the next expedition and able to provide useful character references to any regulars who saw fit to demand them. Essential ingredients of a close-knit community wary of unwarranted interruptions.

So, The Case of the Unknown Soldier came as an alarming diversion when the days turned warmer and early April sunlight shone on the straggling drifts of bluebells in the wood where adventure called. We caught the glint of his jangling medals as he disappeared over the ditch marking the usual boundary for our edge-of-village excursions. A scarred patch under a burgeoning beech tree betrayed efforts to build a fire, while Tubby got excited on finding a sack-blanket crumpled nearby. A heady cocktail of admiration, imagination and fear – he might realise we were mere lads and return to reclaim his ground – sent us scurrying home. We vowed to take another look tomorrow and to keep our discovery secret.

Of course, by the time we crept back into the wood a lone soldier had turned into a fearsome battalion armed to the teeth and a small black patch into a massive encampment. Ernie kept on about tanks, bazookas, prisoners-of-war and invading forces. Tubby said we ought to organise a cricket match instead and ask all the men who used to be in the local Home Guard to take over from us. That's what they were trained for. I suggested we keep quiet and take a quick peep under that beech tree. No need to go right up to it. We could see clearly from behind this bush, but don't let the brambles scratch your legs...

"Hullo, lads. Another nature-study ramble?"

Roadside repairs... a travelling tinker mends a kettle as curious village youngsters look on.

We turned white and rigid all over, three little ice sculptures rooted beneath fingers of sun poking through branches growing heavy with green. Tubby was first to melt, swivelling towards the voice with panic in his eyes and throat. An eerie mixture of moans, mutterings and tears alerted Ernie to imminent danger of tanks and bazookas. As he ducked, and Tubby kept on pleading for mercy, I ran blindly for reinforcements. The man with medals untangled me from the brambles, stifled a chortle and wondered if we'd like a nice cup of tea. Sorry, he didn't have any sugar, but we looked sweet enough.

He was a 'gentleman of the road'. It sounded so much more romantic than a tramp, although I still preferred my father's description of 'milestone inspector' for the occasional passer-by heading for the next workhouse. Dad lifted his hoe in salute from the sugarbeet acres. We sipped khaki tea from an old tin mug under a spreading beech tree.

As warriors went, he was a bit of a disappointment; well-spoken, benign and without bullets or hand grenades in his belt. But that broad smile bearing down on those impressive medals suggested he was ready for tougher battles than out-manoeuvring a trio of woodland cadets trying to earn their spying stripes.

From that adventure on, every unfamiliar figure passing across our village landscape was scrutinised even more intently. If medals, proud and sparkling, were on parade we thought of the Unknown Soldier and felt strangely secure.

A railway refuge

I thought it sounded like the perfect attacking line in seasons when soccer teams joyfully played five men up front – Dereham, Wendling, Fransham, Dunham, Swaffham. And I was privileged to wave the flag for seven years on behalf of the neatest little centre-forward in the business.

Great Fransham railway halt, about 20 minutes of determined biking from home on a good day with a fair wind behind you and no stray bullocks or rogue sugarbeet on the way, became an integral part of my grammar school career. It served as cosy refuge from worldly woes, refreshment quarter when I got up too late for breakfast (about three times a week in summer and once a day in winter), rehearsal room for my budding impressions and rehabilitation centre after those horrible big boys thought it amusing to brighten our return trip by letting my satchel off at Dunham and allowing me the pleasure of going on as far as Wendling.

A roaring coal fire in winter was a rich consolation prize at either end of classroom eternities when I seemed anxious to prove that algebra, geometry, chemistry and physics were surplus to require-ments in the post-war curriculum. A kind woman housed just beyond the level crossing gates regularly rescued my bike from a nearby hedge to park it safely in her garage. She watched my morning panic with rare compassion. Ronnie and Bassie, the ever-cheerful Fransham clerks, did their best to disrupt the British Rail timetable when they saw me approaching, knees pumping, cheeks bursting, cap quivering, bell dinging and reputation glowing for cutting it rather fine. Men working along the track shared tea and yarns around the fire as afternoons folded early and I was reluc-tant to give one of them another chance to trot out his thin line about the 'Swaffham Pedaller'. He persisted with this dreadful pun even after I told him I came from Beeston and had never taken my trusty steed into town.

There were no funny lines from maths master George Moore, scourge of miscreants like me who headed for Hamond's Grammar School under illusions that Pythagoras might be the name of a pop group or Greek footballer who got his angles all wrong. Mr Moore – called 'Mickey' by all, but never to his face – would not suffer fools in his lessons. He twitched his moustache, smoothed his sleek, dark hair, hitched his gown like a giant bat and fixed the unfortunate pupil with a stare designed to curdle milk still lurking in its crate.

Now, I hardly rated as cream at the top of the form and squirmed in total embarrassment many times when fervent prayers to be left alone in my ignorance went unheeded. "Now, Skipper me lad, you've got the genius to illuminate our darkness... ". A complete series of power-cuts later I took extreme measures to avoid retribution for failing to see the point of geometry homework. I sought a measure of relief in the outside lavatory at Fransham railway halt. I spent the whole day hauling my trousers up and down in sub-zero temperatures, an old Norfolk exercise to stop your hypotenuse freezing up. (See, I was listening some of the time).

They came down swiftly when I thought someone was approaching.

I really got the wind up when Ronnie pretended to be Mr Briers, the ever-vigilant school bike inspector, banging on the door to ask why I had bent spokes in my back wheel. Ronnie returned as his jovial self after dinner, loudly thanking his wife for "the best apple pie I have ever tasted". My stomach rumbled. The rest of me shuddered as my asylum continued.

I biked home in gathering darkness to face the music, a short concerto in three sudden movements – confession, a ding of the lug and bed. It was many years before I found enough courage to explain my away-day antics to Mr Moore. I had just opened a fete at Swaffham Cottage Hospital, and we enjoyed several more good-natured mardles, especially at old boys' reunions. He never referred to my blatant shortcomings in subjects he taught with distinction. The milk-curdling stare had mellowed into a sort of forgiving smile.

The old railway line closed over 30 years ago, but wheels keep turning at the Fransham halt. When Bob and Ann Jenkins bought the derelict station house some years back they aimed to renovate it as a holiday home. But then they decided to indulge their hobby of mending old engines, and, occasionally, making new machines. There's plenty of space to house their possessions in a garden which takes in part of the old station yard, a platform with a waiting room, and which then stretches for a quarter of a mile along the old track.

They have worked hard and well to retain that magical railway atmosphere of the buildings opened in 1847. But the outside lavatory has gone. I wonder where errant schoolboys go these days when geometry homework is due but not done...

Railway echoes… along the Dereham-Swaffham line. Staff and young supporters on parade at Wendling during its heyday.

*Hail beauteous **May** that dost inspire,*

Mirth, and youth, and warm desire!

May Musings

Filling pew hours

I glimpsed eternity many times in our village chapel when travelling preachers appeared completely oblivious to joys of the great summer game. The longest sermons, readings and hymns had to be saved for those Sundays when vital confrontations were staged on the cricket meadow just beyond the war memorial not far from the old aerodrome runway.

Neat pencil work and a passion for community life had brought me the post of Saturday scorer with its thrilling but frightening possibility of being asked to fill a gap in the team when farm duties called one of the regulars. 'The boy' went in last, desperately hoping nothing depended upon his batting performance, and fielded where the nettles and cowpats were deepest. My earliest emergency outing was marked by the visitors running five, as I tried to clean the ball with a clump of grass before returning it from the boundary edge.

Sadly, I was but a shadowy figure on the fringes of Sunday action on or off the field, as compulsory chapel attendance restricted involvement to a few stolen minutes of sporting dreams between marathon afternoon and evening services. May was the cruellest month as early-season averages cried out for attention and cup competitions still carried genuine hopes of progress. The weather wore its friendliest smile, a breeze tickling blossoms into confetti showers over green-trimmed lanes under vivid blue skies. I was moved to pray for rain when the fates threw up a Sunday clash with deadly local rivals, Longham. A delay would mean a mid-week rescheduling and a chance for me to preach my usual propaganda about the laws of averages pointing to an overdue Beeston victory.

It was, then, a struggle to pay full and undivided attention to words of wisdom flowing from the pulpit. Thankfully, there were no questions afterwards. Sadly, that policy did not apply to treble physics or double algebra during sun-blessed grammar school days when my mind wandered off towards Old Trafford or Trent Bridge. At least Sunday innings were based on completely parochial consid-erations, a small but important conscience salver as I nodded politely and shook hands with the preacher. And I discovered a glorious path through the tedious undergrowth of the endless sermon. Perhaps I should have patented it for future congregations of all denominations faced with the problem of filling pew time usefully.

Like all supreme ideas, it began accidentally. I was experimenting with a highly complicated game you could play by yourself based on cricket and the Methodist hymn book. It culminated in those most prolific of hymn-writers, brothers Charles and John Wesley, sharing the new ball attack against all the rest. Wickets fell or runs accrued according to the first letter of the verse on which you alighted after opening the book at random. Vowels were fatal for the batsman – 'O God, our help in ages past', 'Abide with me' and 'Immortal love forever full' – while a few consonants brought boundaries. It became far more complex when I introduced a rule concerning the number of verses in a hymn and lbw decisions, stumpings and wides. Suffice to say I never completed a game during one sermon, and I abandoned it because there were too many arguments over which end Charles Wesley should take after lunch.

I turned to the Bible for fresh inspiration, painting a look of surprise on the face of a chapel elder nearby and running my finger along the lines to show I meant business. It stopped as I read something about David's triumph being heard throughout Israel. My imagination shot into overdrive. This was it! The perfect answer to my Sunday somnolence – a hunt for sporting references in the Good Book! Football soon fell to my industrious charge – 'Am I my brother's keeper?' – but I cheated a bit to cover tennis with someone serving in the courts of Pharaoh.

Of course, cricket was the main challenge. I considered lilies of the field, how they grow; they toil not, neither do they spin. I knew there had to be a better line. A school friend, dizzy with excitement on first encountering the wonders of Shakespeare, asked if Henry V could help out with his observation, 'I see you stand like greyhounds in the slips'. But I told him to make up his own game.

Then, just as I was about to move on to horse racing and hockey, one of those everlasting preachers in the parish pulpit provided the answer. Good job I was half-listening as he shared the story of Jesus and his disciples on the Sea of Tiberias when fish were scarce. A happy ending came when their nets bulged. My joy was complete as they toiled in the deep and caught nothing.

I beamed at the preacher. He seemed a little bemused at my sudden conversion to full-time attention. Then he smiled back in acceptance that little miracles could happen on a sunny Sunday afternoon.

Ahead of my time

While the farmyard scene inspired acres of admiration and affection, I sensed my connections might be confined to distant headlands as soon as some decent examination results cropped up. With father, two elder brothers and countless other relatives and friends so close to the land, it seemed Norfolk agriculture could well survive without my puny efforts.

To be frank, I was more of a dreamer than a doer, and that made me an easy target for the earthy elite always ready to rehearse a chorus of rural abuse. The tractor clutch slipped as often as my reputation. I didn't relish getting my hands dirty or squelching through piles of steaming manure. I complained regularly of giddiness while singling sugar beet behind the flashing hoes of men on piecework. I could not master the art of coaxing cows safely in and out of the milking shed. I kept my distance at threshing time when rats were goaded out of hiding. I was scared of geese as well. Hardly surprising, then, that I was never fully accepted by the hard-working, level-headed folk around me. They put up with a skinny interloper mainly because they knew he was going back to school soon, or – and this prompted lengthy celebrations behind his aching back – he had landed a pen-pushing job miles from their fields coated in honest sweat and toil.

It was much more in relief than shame that I bade farewell to a world to which I simply was not suited. That was half the battle won, accepting my limitations and getting well out of the way before I could wreak more damage. The farm was no place for someone frightened of hard work, good muck, tractors, rats, geese...

So how come I managed to find so much to admire and like through long Saturday mornings and everlasting holidays? Why did my ill-starred stint as a son of the soil leave such a deep impression? What drove innermost feelings way beyond guilt at not being equipped to continue a proud family tradition? As usual, my closest village confidants, Tubby, Ernie and Rodney, helped find useful answers to difficult questions at one of our final hedgerow conferences before fate, opportunity and ambition sent us off in different directions.

"You've always been ahead of your time", said Tubby consolingly as I contemplated departure.

"Yeh," interjected Ernie. "You wanted to go home before the others had hardly started!"

Rodney couldn't top that one, so he turned the debate gently towards sex education and our inestimable good fortunes at being brought up in such an enlightened time and place. We had picked up a host of handy words and expressions to help us come to terms with dramatic physical and emotional changes. Listening to the men and watching the animals was better than any encyclopaedia or evening classes behind the bikeshed.

I had read enough D.H. Lawrence novels to be aware of all kinds of romantic notions about being close to nature, early-morning ping of milk in pail, sap rising in dew-laden meadows and certain answers lying in the soil. We had paid sixpence often enough to take a doe rabbit to a neighbour's foot-stamping buck, and watched a bull being ushered towards bovine delights, to realise this whole getting-together business could be perfectly straightforward and less embarrassing than many well-meaning people suggested. Perhaps the Swinging Sixties had yet to claim us, but we knew there was a giant pendulum somewhere beyond the fertilised crops.

While I did not have the temerity to class myself a victim of encroaching mechanisation – I was of little use even before it started encroaching – I suspected some sort of revolution was gaining momentum after the horses had been put out to grass and the binders left in the shade by roaring combines. Without really knowing why, I started to take more notice of the way men tackled seasonal tasks

– the mud-crusted rhythm of knockin' and toppin' sugar beet, the firm-footed dance involved in building a perfect stack, the matchless tapestry of the thatcher's strawed temple, harvest's crowning glory in the setting sun. All arts beyond my scope, but admiration grew as they became more specialised and less familiar.

I retain deep respect for those who work the land, a dwindling army in a fast-changing countryside. I am thankful now that I had the chance to get close to a farming era built on far more muscle, purpose and dedication than I could muster. At least it has ensured me a reasonably comfortable seat at 'fourses time' to listen to masters of rural literature like John Stewart Collis, Henry Williamson and Adrian Bell. Working writers who had to scrub mud from their hands before picking up the evening pen.

Now that's real overtime in the old quest for a straight furrow.

Frolics on the farm... but challenges of the countryside didn't suit all those called to face them.

Horse power...
ploughman Sidney Knights
of Hemsby with two
hardworking colleagues.

Doing a turn

My current role as leader of the travelling Press Gang entertainers, unashamed purveyors of home-made mirth, mardling and melody, owes much to a series of old-fashioned social evenings in the Nissen hut that served as our village hall after the last war.

While dressing up and performing impromptu epics were regular features of the classroom, and our Sunday School anniversary provided an ideal platform for those who relished reciting to a full house, it took more relaxed community capers to make me part of a generation willing and able to make its own amusement. Television had yet to imprison families in their own homes after tea – indeed, electricity was still a novelty – and doing a turn came naturally to people who knew each other's strengths and weaknesses inside out. Familiarity bred contempt for those afraid to join in any homespun fun. And children adored the idea of grown-ups being silly just for the sake of it.

I recall one social fling when various pillars of our rural society, including the rector, parish council chairman and a farmer hitherto better known as 'the most miserable old beggar ever to tramp a ten-acre field', prompted torrents of applause with amusing verses and monologues. Lew Dack, a farmer of more amiable repute, sang You Are My Sunshine, and really meant it when his wife was persuaded to stand up in the audience and lead a mass joining-in for the final chorus. Shopkeeper Ted Margarson told yarns I'd heard pass over the counter with margarine, sausages and aniseed balls just a week or so before. Queenie Laws, with a dash of eccentricity that made her a popular choice to top the bill, had us cheering and chanting an animated impression of The Village Pump. No shortage of young volunteers to operate her handle as laughter flowed. We were reluctant to let go, not just because the act was so good but because her exit meant another night of spontaneous gaiety was over. "Perhaps you lads would like to give us an item of your own next time" produced a heady cocktail of fear and excitement as we headed home from the palace of varieties on the old aerodrome.

Next day's hastily convened meeting of the entertainments sub-committee in our secret hideout half way between the lilypits and the top of Red Barn Hill carried a majority decision. I proposed Tubby, Ernie and Rodney should join me to write and present a sketch culminating in a song at the next social gathering. They proposed it should be a solo offering, and they would do the scenery, prompting and advertising. Such generous and adventurous support inspired me to new heights of creation, although I was tempted to reconsider my oft-quoted maxim that 'everybody can do something on stage'. Ernie suggested wetting yourself was no automatic passport to the Old Vic or London Palladium.

Perhaps I was a bit of a show-off, blessed with a useful memory, good sense of timing and the sort of imagination needed to rise above mundane chores dished out constantly to a family of ten children. My excuses for not cleaning shoes, folding clothes, making the bed, doing errands or feeding the rabbits may have bordered on the bizarre, but at least they bought me time to consider follow-up subterfuge if needed to avoid a clip round the ear. Eventually I treated accusations of "talking a lot of old squit" as a clear indica-tion that hopes of a career in showbusiness were coming on nicely.

Squit… such a precious local commodity, nonsense, light-hearted foolery, but usually accompanied by a half-admiring smile or friendly nod and invariably carrying an entertaining edge. I felt it my destiny to be counted among the Norfolk yarn-tellers, holding court, maybe relating the same old stories but managing to make them sound fresh, especially when new, unsuspecting listeners joined the audience.

A world premiere of a one-boy sketch on the rickety stage at the Nissen hut on Beeston aerodrome fed such ambitions in the 1950s. Heading the Press Gang team of squit merchants round the county (and occasionally beyond) since the mid-1980s, as well as singing for my supper at countless local events, underlines the value of those early stints in village vaudeville. The biggest compliment we can receive at our nights of Norfolk bonhomie is to be told: "Do you know, that was just like the old social get-togethers we used to have years ago."

Homemade pantomime fun points to an upsurge of that old-style community spirit in our village halls, and I have noted many other heartening examples on my rural rounds. It may be the chap on the microphone spicing up the raffle draw; the mawther lured into the spotlight to give 'em a song at the end of a social do; the committee member bribed into telling the only local joke fit for the parson's ears; the parson going one better. Of-the-cuff fun, with relative newcomers – in the village for less than 20 years – making their pitch as the mood mellows.

Droll model for all who feel Norfolk humour can still be elevated to an art form must be Sidney Grapes, alias The Boy John. He enjoyed local celebrity for many years as a dialect comedian before he wrote his first letter to the Eastern Daily Press in 1946 and introduced all those memorable country characters to a wide band of readers. He gloried in the part of the rustic who wasn't such a fool as he looked. The audience would be laughing at him halfway through a yarn. By the time he'd got to the punchline, they were laughing with him.

That was the essential format when the Beeston cast took our mind off boring post-war matters like rationing, hydrogen bombs and mains sewerage with a few dollops of squit. I can still hear and see them daring their audience to get there first, and then milking the golden moment as they finished together in a gale of laughter.

Droll model for all Norfolk squit merchants. Rustic comedian Sidney Grapes, alias The Boy John, holding court on the village hall stage.

June damp and warm

Does the farmer no harm.

June Junkets

Coronation Stakes

June soon has me busting out all over in a rash of boyhood guilt. It stems from an egg-and-spoon race on Lew Dack's buttercup-decked meadow, the Coronation Stakes of 1953. I cheated, thumb firmly on egg for all but the last few yards of the village charge for a shiny new sixpence.

They cheered, I smiled and fell over deliberately in the sack race. That coin became a lead weight in my pocket for the rest of the summer. I just could not let go of the feeling that I had won by foul means. For all I know, others may have employed equally shadowy tactics or even smuggled chewing gum beneath the shell. But I had triumphed, and it wasn't fair.

The sixpence glinted at me accusingly as I placed it alongside my Coronation Bible and mug, presented in a lather of memorable ceremonials at the village school. 'Do no sinful actions, speak no angry words' rang out the assembly anthem, and I was sorely tempted to take the first slice of advice rather personally. Every minor diversion from the straight and narrow had me racked with remorse, and I cultivated a glowing reputation for being magnanimous in defeat and ultra-modest in not coming last.

The village Coronation fancy dress competition could have been a painful affair had I not been so anxious to make amends for under-hand scheming on Lew Dack's meadow. I made a good jockey in my orange and purple silks, and the judges had to be impressed by a high-pitched whinny, even-paced canter and delicate use of the whip. I was ready with all the salient details of Gordon Richards' first Derby win on Pinza. Frankly, I was furlongs ahead of the rest of the field when it came to living the part, right down to smacking my backside and calling "Giddyup, ole bewty!" when we were asked to parade.

I came third behind Snow White and Robin Hood. Jack, with an apology for a beanstalk made out of school milk bottle tops, and a grizzly bear who had wet himself while waiting to roar followed me on a lap of honour. There was no stewards' inquiry, although my best mates and trainers, Tubby and Ernie, said they simply could not understand why I had not won. I let them into a little secret. The chief adjudicator, a parish worthy scarcely noted for his sense of humour, had tried to engage all contestants in a gentle question-and-answer session. Most of his inquiries prompted quivering lips and shakes of the head. I knew extra marks were there for the taking with a few bold replies:

"Ah, the sport of kings. And in which race do we find you, my young man?"

"The human race."

"That's not quite what I meant, but we'll let that pass. What is the name of your mount?"

"Dusty Carpet."

"Dusty Carpet? Why do you call him Dusty Carpet?"

"Because he'll take a lot of beating."

He didn't ask any more questions. The look on his face suggested I would be very fortunate to finish up in the winner's enclosure. Much of the guilt I had carried since victory in the egg-and-spoon stakes went into that daring repartee. It might have been wasted on the chief adjudicator, but he helped me along the rocky road of penitence. I congratulated Snow White and Robin Hood, forgoing any references to little men or merrie outlaws, and commiserated with Jack, who had thrown his pathetic beanstalk away, and a very damp bear eager to get back to his lair.

There were other opportunities to do penance that summer. I owned up to wrecking the Sword Dance in the school playground, even though two other boys had been equally as clumsy with their thrusts into the middle. I accepted a highly debatable decision without a grouse on the orchard Test Match arena after scoring 93 runs and preparing myself mentally for the first century of a fluctuating career. I smiled benevolently when Snow White got higher marks than me for a composition about How We Celebrated The Coronation.

I even made the chief adjudicator feel good at not pushing my case in the fancy dress handicap. We came face to face in the village shop two weeks later...

"Ah, the little jockey who came home third. And what's the latest from the course, my young man?"

"Water Tap is still running."

A youngster **celebrating** at the village Coronation party.

Playing in the road

Today's truculent traffic mocks memories of lanes, meadows and people ambling gently to nowhere in particular. A blast of the horn, a roar of the engine and a mimed expletive or two soon put paid to any sentimental nonsense about loitering over yesterday's rural perambulations...

Is it safe to come out of the hemlock and hogweed? Now I can see them mowing grasses in the prime of their bloom under a fair June sky as the scent floats across shorn fields. Cocks of sweet hay stand in rough rank. Partridges, rabbits and many other creatures must now head for cover in nearby forests of burgeoning corn.

A busy pastoral picture, but there's time to savour all colours and sounds as the more florid pageantry of summer arrives. Wild roses blush in hedgerows and poppy red runs along the banks and the green aisles of the wheat. First white lilies lie at the heart of the pit where winter's frosts produced a precarious skating rink for the parish's more daring exhibitionists. I was not among them after nightmarish dreams about hobnailed boots and splintering ice.

Rooks in the rectory trees have their young, and harsh voices are softened. Bumble bees sip and hum among purple clover flowers. Rat, vole, field mouse, hedgehog and shrew rustle hither and thither; all are hunting, and most are hunted. The cuckoo changes his tune to a stuttering call and the songs of the nightingale are fading from the coppices. The little water-course at the foot of Red Barn Hill gurgles again after a sudden shower.

Nature in its pomp, with Sunday evening after church and chapel prime time for communal inspection. Farmers, workers and anyone else passing size up crops. Frowns and smiles sum up expectations, although care is taken not to give best to neighbours bound to make capital out of any misgivings cast over blossoming acres.

I recall a leading agricultural figure from a nearby village paying a sort of rustic state visit to join our after-sermon stroll in the 1950s. Flanked by two of his men, and sporting a Sunday buttonhole as big as a saucer, he snorted, pointed, chuckled and then disappeared as swiftly as he came. He didn't utter a word, but we knew what he thought of our harvest prospects compared to his own. Perhaps he repeated the exercise in other villages, but I considered it rude and swanky to take such a derisory stance. Tubby said it was probably because he had been beaten in his local flower and vegetable show. Ernie thought he'd had a row with one of our farmers before the war, and this was his way of showing fences had yet to be mended.

Such disruptions were rare as communities looked forward to the coronation of the year, parochial pride forming the right kind of avenue for timeless processions. The road lengthmen tidied verges, unclogged ditches and swept up little hills of debris formed by leaf-lifting breezes long before the hurricanes and mountains of a throwaway age.

Playing in the road was hardly a hazardous alternative to Lord's and Wembley pitches we carved out of buttercup-flecked pastures next door to where Tubby's dad kept his pigs or the well-stocked orchard separating my old homestead from the highway. As long as one of the players combined traffic patrol with sporting duties, and was prepared to forfeit an innings at the crease or a chance to shine from the penalty spot, we had plenty of time to clear the way. "Here come Alec on his tractor!" and "Six on'em on hosses from the riding school!" were regular preludes to removal of all obstacles. We stood in an unlikely huddle of order and politeness, giving the distinct impression of never having seen a tractor or a horse before.

Occasionally, a favourite arena was hijacked by the tar lorry, all bubble and squeak with chippings for afters. We followed at a safe distance while a familiar surface got a smart new look, but temptation reared its sticky head as soon as the workmen had gone. A turpentine bath would have come in useful to restore a bunch of Al Jolson lookalikes to something near Norfolk respectability before anxious confessions at bedtime.

Our young world was generally quieter, safer, slower and cleaner, with June's growing glories demanding spells of overtime in lane and loke. As we got older, traffic multiplied and became louder, faster and destroyer of soft musings and sporting interludes around the hemlock and hogweed.

Just in time to make a modicum of sense out of education's insistence that this most inviting of months should be laden with evening hours of revision and days of classroom examination while summer ripened and rioted outside. The road to enlightenment was paved with long detentions.

The Bridge, Filby Broad, near

Norfolk roads wore a quieter and friendlier look before traffic began its incessant charge. There's plenty of room here to saunter across the bridge at Filby Broad.

Genuine characters

If we don't get country characters like we used to, perhaps we ought to point the finger at local cooling rather than global warming. It is much harder these days to stand out in the Norfolk crowd unless behaviour lurches towards the utterly bizarre. While the media in general and television in particular, constantly glorify daft antics and suggest blatant exhibitionism is normal and healthy, it seems perfectly reasonable to peer into yesterday's hedgerows for a few sprigs of genuine rustic behaviour.

Such are the pace of life and rate of change that traditional virtues like dry humour, local pride and mild xenophobia can be missed altogether. Subtle lines of communication that once drew native and newcomer closer while still confusing the casual visitor – "Never yew mind where I live, dew yew come an' see me" – have been choked up by lottery hard-luck stories and arguments over Received Pronunciation. Mobile phones have replaced mardling. Nonconformists are thin on the ground.

The very idea of village worthies holding court on the memorial seat under the spreading chestnut tree outside the old forge draws guffaws of mocking laughter. Jeremy Clarkson soundalikes are drowning out quaint echoes of the past. Rolling acres of fertile farmland used to reverberate with rough and ready humour when workers knew they had to provide their own fun or go without. Now a lone ploughman clambers into his air-conditioned tractor cab, checks the computer and turns the cassette over for Vivaldi in season.

When I was a lad (and how my sons cheer when I hoist that signal for a stroll down memory loke!) it seemed every village was an ideal stage for real characters, some endearing themselves to more orthodox members of a small society by dint of eccentric manner-isms or dress. I reckon a fair number to make a memorable mark ended up doing or saying things simply because it was expected of them, especially when yarns flowed along with ale at the pub.

For all that, most outstanding personalities from my growing-up years in Beeston are urged forward to take a bow out of simple respect and affection. They all wore ready smiles, but could muster reproachful glances if needed. They all knew how far children tried to push their luck, but never discouraged the budding spirit of adventure behind such tactics. They all made you feel special when it really mattered without pretending or patronising. In short, they understood the generation game and the rules that shaped and ran it in a small country community just after the last war.

Schoolteachers Mrs Tann and Mrs Webdale turned countless rough little pieces of ground into promising allotments. Chapel Sunday School superintendent Harry Dawson and his wife Alice, who looked after the smaller children, cultivated a spiritual corner after clearing away brambles of doubt and derision. Bertha Naylor, a parson's widow who returned to the village to look after her aged parents, played the Chapel organ and led several of us from the Garden of Eden to scripture examination success.

Elijah Dickerson cared for the war memorial on the edge of the old aerodrome from where so many young Americans had flown out for the last time. Flowers nodded remembrance over carefully shorn grass. Elijah read the inscription for us when we stopped on the way home from games along the runway. He told us about a war that had tied little Beeston to the USA.

May Burrell, a retired nurse who had also revived village links to care for an elderly relative, and Mildred Symonds both rode sit-up-and-beg bicycles. They were erect pillars of the Parish Church – Mildred taught at the Church Sunday School – but both displayed a generous ecumenical streak when Chapel hedgerow raiders called at the door with plump blackberries. May, brusque, fast-talking and permanently on the edge of a knowing chuckle, ordered all youngsters to do something useful with spare time. Mildred, gentle, softly-spoken and regularly fussing towards a packed larder, appeared content to let her industrious example act as sufficient inspiration.

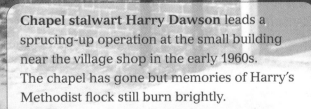

Chapel stalwart Harry Dawson leads a
sprucing-up operation at the small building
near the village shop in the early 1960s.
The chapel has gone but memories of Harry's
Methodist flock still burn brightly.

Contrasting characters with similar amounts of time to invest in children.

Auntie May, as she was invariably known, took on the mantle of medical all-rounder, delivering babies, tending the sick and laying out the departed. Her matter-of-fact manner often belied a deeply-caring and sensitive nature... although she had every right to let rip the night tipsy customers from the Bell pub opposite her home in The Street decided to test her nursing credentials to the hilt. Wilfred Cross was persuaded to 'collapse and moan' on her front doorstep while deeply concerned colleagues threw gravel at a bedroom window and called for May's assistance. By the time she'd dressed and hurried downstairs to make a swift diagnosis, the victim had made a miraculous recovery and rejoined a raucous, rolling band of Bullards beer-tasters heading for the next jolly jape.

My country cavalcade of colourful personalities could easily stretch from village shop in the middle to remote farmhouse on the parish boundary. Yes, I did know everyone by name and nature. Of course, that meant they knew all about me. Perhaps such familiarity was at the core of a brand of trust and respect sadly diluted since by extra speed, size and shameless insularity.

*Hot **July** brings cooling showers*
Apricots and gillyflowers.

July Jaunts

Life's rich cycle

A sensibly-integrated transport system blessed out country routes when I was a lad. Of course, we didn't need to travel so far in those days and in any case it was more fun waiting for Danes, Vikings and itinerants from Norwich way to fall foul of our labyrinth of lanes and lokes. Now and again we admitted the war might be over and turned signposts round to give reasonable directions, but a sudden gust in the night could cause havoc in the morning if a new lorry driver was collecting full milk churns from outlying farms. Curdled tempers down yesterday's rutted drifts surely opened a path to road rage antics of today.

Walking and cycling were the main means of getting round the parish and a few miles beyond, although the pony and trap lingered on as a colourful alternative especially among small-time dealers and full-time imbibers who relied on sheer animal instinct to deliver them home safely after a lengthy session at the bar. It has been claimed, with some justification, that our shrewdest four-legged friends played a vital role in supporting the rural pubs network before the age of breathalysers and crowded roads. Horsepitality at a canter.

There was a regular bus service into town, for shoppers and workers during the week and for fleshpot-seekers on a Saturday night. Amazing how temptation tasted so much sweeter seven miles from home. Carter's Coaches of Litcham widened many mid-Norfolk horizons before and after the Festival of Britain, even if the height of daring rested on singing alternative lyrics to the latest Guy Mitchell hit on the back seat returning from Dereham.

When I became the first boy in the village to pass the eleven-plus examination – an achievement not entirely unrelated to the fact I was the first boy in the village to have a pencil – a double delight eased the trail to faraway Swaffham. The educational authorities provided me with my first proper bike to eat up the miles between the old homestead and Fransham Railway Station, where I caught the appropriate train when punctures, powerful head winds and Test Matches did not intervene. The last-mentioned could play havoc with my timetable as England's brave cricketers reached a crucial stage in the series and demanded my undivided attention. Thursday morning afflictions, savage stomach pains, excruciating headaches, prolonged dizzy turns and anything else that couldn't be seen, reached a seasonal peak in July.

I forced myself out of bed to twiddle the wireless knobs and check the accumulator just before play started. My remarkable run of 11.28am recoveries mocked all known medical knowledge, but owed much to my dear mother's cheerful refusal to become a slave to the clock or the calendar. She never noticed the uncanny coincidences linking her stricken boy with fresh international showdowns at Trent Bridge, Lord's and Old Trafford. Even so, I felt bad enough about such charlatan behaviour to make certain I did all errands without prompting the following weekend.

For the first golden term of seven grammar school years I savoured the timeless joys of steam train travel. It would have been even more wonderful if bigger lads in our compartment – and that meant all the others – hadn't seen fit to tie the tiddler to the luggage rack in the hope of rendering him slightly taller by the end of the journey. Such bold experiments in the name of pioneering genetic engineering ended with the arrival of diesel locomotives, open-plan, functional and scourge of all schoolboys with a flair for individuality and traditional fun.

Happily, my bike continued to make inroads into uncharted territory. I was a late developer, and while other youthful saps rose in harmony with springtime symphonies, my romantic inclinations seemed to come to the boil in July as corn ripened, holidays beckoned and girls wore less. Cousin Veronica, who lived in the same village, often had Dereham High School colleagues staying at weekends. One in particular set my heart pounding with her knowing smile, auburn tresses and rosy cheeks. Way out of my class, to be sure, but she might just be a little bit impressed by a sustained show of rustic athleticism. I put that theory to the test with a high-powered series of pedalling feats past Veronica's house.

The girls were outside when I roared in for my 58th lap. They probably emerged on hearing my grunts while pink knees wobbled with tiredness and sweat soaked my shirt. I tried a casual wave and nonchalant smile, lost my balance, crashed into the bank opposite and ended in an undignified heap. The only impression I made was on my left knee and rear wheel.

Exit red-faced Romeo, sadly unaware of how certain episodes had to be treated as one more spoke in life's rich cycle. Still, it was a racing certainty I would conduct future sizing-up missions with less haste and more due care and attention.

More leisurely times on our roads when horse and cart and bicycle dominated the picture. The young lad in this scene appears to be keeping an eye out for unwanted intruders – or was he just trying to impress the young lady out for a ride on her trusty steed?

Tall stories

Those three old boys up the corner playing dominoes and sipping a half of the summer mild can no longer anticipate red-carpet treatment down at Ye Olde Dewdrop Inne. While a booming tourist trade in the county where young Horatio Nelson surely learnt how to talk proper must peer into yesterday's hedgerows for a few sprigs of rustic heritage, we know we'll think far more of the dear old Norfolk character when he's been consigned to history. As someone's old granny used to say: "Yew dunt really miss it 'til yew hent got it" – and she wasn't talking about her ration book.

I recall with relish a host of colourful personalities parading through my boyhood of the 1950s. One old chap on the farm where my father worked convinced me he had discovered a cow's nest. Following him in full expectation of extending my grasp of nature study beyond the bikeshed academy, I had the good sense to laugh as he unravelled six empty milk bottles in the hedge.

That was by no means the last time I fell for a spot of homely leg-pulling, but it did put me on my guard when the harvest army asked for volunteers to fetch a pail of dry water or a tin of striped paint. And I really knew that making the wire netting slope was no guarantee of keeping rain off the chickens. We more worldly lads simply smirked as the latest recruit to our agricultural scene was asked if he wanted an odd job. A reply in the affirmative drew this side-splitting offer: "Right, boy, go an' milk the bull... thass an odd job!"

Squit among the haystacks was a useful preparation for a scrawny boy with literary ambitions. "Sharpen yar wits as well as yar pencil!" called that old chap with a proclivity for finding things in the hedge as I walked away one late-summer's morning. I exacted some measure of revenge a few years later with the tallest story I could find when we met for a mardle in the village pub where his japes had assumed legendary levels.

It concerned a man who could get you anything. They used to call them higglers or 'little do-ers' in Norfolk. One day, two smart-looking gents approached our rural all-rounder in the pub and said they wanted a hare for coursing. He promised to get them one within hours.

He caught one, killed it, skinned it and then sewed the skin on a cat. He put the cat in a cage and sent a message to the men that he had indeed managed to obtain them a hare. "Bring your dogs," he said. They did, and the party went to the bottom of a field, this chap with the 'hare' in a sack. When he let it go, they released their dogs. It went straight up a tree.

I was doing well to keep a straight face as the yarn reached its climax: "These gentlemen had never seen a hare climb up a tree before. For all I know, they're still trying to make their friends believe it."

My old colleague on the farm was lost for words. So I bought him a pint. I thought of him fondly not long ago on discovering the art of telling tall stories has not been smothered entirely by the dull blanket of uniformity. For example, this one surfaced in a hostelry where customers are not afraid to laugh either at or with each other.

Fred told Billy his hens laid two eggs a day each. "Well," said Billy, "When I wuz in the Navy in the Med an' we hed a day orf, some on'us went swimmin'. We dived an' found an old Spanish galleon. On the stern wuz tew gret big lanterns wi' the candles still alight."

"Dunt talk such squit!" exclaimed Fred.

"Right yew are," said Billy. "Yew half yar egg production, an' I'll blow my candles out!"

Country characters found plenty of time for colourful yarns along with leg-pulling when the pace of Norfolk life was much slower.

Knickerbocker glory

I have yet to master the social art of dancing, a gap in my education which may help explain regular overtime sessions of mardling at or near the bar on my Norfolk rounds. There's simply no choice when the hunt is on for likely partners to share the delights of a foxtrot, quickstep, tango or rumba. I can slouch a waltz as long as I don't have to lead, and, in weaker moments, prance about for one of those non-contact, free-for-all frolics designed to fill the floor with reluctant renegades. But as a rule, when the Come Dancing lights beckon, I've gone missing.

Reckon it all began the day Mum decked me out in that soppy outfit for the schools' country dancing festival at Litcham. Usually, a bus trip out of the village with your mates was cause for eager anticipation. This one had to be purgatory on wheels as I looked at myself in the wardrobe mirror. A checked blouse, billowing and buttoned up tight at the top with strict instructions to keep it that way, and navy blue knickerbockers that did my little pink knees no fashion favours whatsoever. Who on earth would even bother to admire my brand new white plimsolls while they feasted disbelieving eyes on that outrageous uniform above? I swallowed hard, cursed our cultural heritage and took the long way to school in order to avoid bumping into people I knew.

My track record suggested I would avoid the call-up. Commitment to the team ethic had been seriously questioned by a whole series of blunders on rehearsal laps for the accursed Sword Dance. I poked instead of pulled, or pulled instead of poked, as a star-like pattern emerged above our gyrating bodies. The big moment crumbled into chaos. No need for a playground inquest. Scarlet cheeks, hunched shoulders and the hole waiting to swallow me up near the railings pointed to yet another Skipper-inspired failure. I fared little better in dances that had no props, frantic cavortings hamstrung by a telling impression of two left feet in hobnailed boots.

No wonder I enjoyed more space than anyone else. I was volunteered so often to operate the gramophone that I drifted automatically into the wings when stepping-out lessons arrived.

So, it came as a big surprise to us all when my name appeared on the list of performers for the area festival. The fact there were no other boys to select from may have forced our teachers' hands, but such niceties meant nothing as I confronted the challenge of forcing my legs and brain to do what did not come naturally. I fully intended to skulk and sulk the awful day away. A masterstroke of pupil management changed my tune as we clambered aboard the bus.

I had been paired with Marina Dunn, one of our best dancers and, by common consent, one of nature's more desirable creatures, for this special occasion when the school's prowess would be put to the test on 'foreign' floorboards. I felt sick with fear and excitement as she sat beside me and said I looked really smart. She may have meant, "Oh, God, look what I've been lumbered with!" or "How am I supposed to camouflage this clumsy clot's weaknesses?" but the smile and motherly attitude helped drown out catcalls from jealous chums at the back. I had arrived as a romantic force to be reckoned with. Now all I needed was divine inspiration to develop twinkling toes for a few hours and they could hold the front page for Norfolk's twirling answer to Fred Astaire and Ginger Rogers…

Perhaps it turned out to be more like Trigger and Roy Rogers as I champed at the bit, pawed the ground and tried to follow gentle coaxing of my patient mentor. The biggest factor in my favour was the number of performers on parade, making it much easier than usual to hide my obvious shortcomings. I could even pretend the odd gallop came quite instinctively, and I was strangely heartened by the sight of lads from other village squads struggling to stay true to the pace and rhythm of familiar strains. My partner nursed me through more intricate numbers, but she was relatively powerless as we reached the Sword Dance finale with all its teamwork requirements. I braced myself for a supreme artistic effort. Dread and adrenaline were my partners now. They saw me through without calamity.

That ordeal took so much out of me, physically and emotionally, I was oblivious to comments of all colours on the way home. Marina seemed satisfied at coming through unscathed, although I had steered uncertain feet to go where previous partners had feared to tread. While no-one in authority picked me out for special praise – possibly aware that bad old habits would resurface at the following week's playground romp – I had to be grateful for not being cited as the perfect example of what happens when you don't eat your greens or show co-ordination when it matters.

Suffice to suggest this was the high point of my dancing career, a summer's day when I defied predictions of disaster thanks, in no small part, to a girl who accepted she had drawn the short straw. Her reward? Never to be saddled with me again. She showed true gratitude by refusing to make classroom capital out of a festival fling with a nifty little mover in all his blouse-and-knickerbocker glory.

Four pretty maids from North Walsham way show poise to go with their high-stepping enthusiasm.

*If **August** 24th be fair and clear,*

Hope for a prosperous autumn that year.

August Antics

Chasing the rabbits

August is the cruellest month when it comes to a crop of embarrassing memories. As the dog-rose nods us towards another Harvest Home, I flinch at the sound of combines churning across seas of golden corn, the sight of dew glinting on stubble fields and the smell of oil mingling with dust and crackling straw.

It seems most of my youthful shortcomings were pinned on that familiar country canvas for all to scrutinise while the oldest festival engaged entire communities for a few hectic weeks. Binder and sheaves, elevator and jugs of beer, children waving sticks and chasing rabbits, real and imaginary, into that patch left in the middle… yes, the coronation of the year had real majesty as stacks rose like temples in the setting sun and a cooling breeze ruffled the last load of the day.

But all I can hear drifting across the headlands of time is a chorus of rural abuse as the tractor clutch slipped. Members of an earthy elite loading the harvest on the trailer behind lurched and yelled, threatening to cut off my supply of Woodbines if they should happen to survive. They promised far more drastic punishment after the stack-wrecking saga up Red Barn Hill. Tractor troubles reached a pique when confusion arose between clutch and brake. I was guilty of a simple misjudgement en route to the elevator. One corner of the fast-growing stack was taken out. The other three started to sag along with my reputation as a useful lad to have around at this time of the year. Banishment to a distant hedgerow on that steamy August afternoon left me on the verge of complete retirement from farming chores. I continued only through a burning desire to delay what was bound to be a derisory farewell collection.

As one who started harvest duties with an acceptance that horse-power was much safer when the horses had it, I always preferred to treat it as an archaic rite rather than a mechanical process. The transition from Snowball the Suffolk Punch with unflappable temperament to Fordson Major with kangaroo clutch and brake was a painful one. I had been warned you couldn't shout "Whoa!" or " Howdgee!" to a tractor. Well, you could, but it tended not to take any notice. Not that I struck up the smoothest of relationships with all farmyard creatures.

I was outmanoeuvred by cows in the dairy to the extent of losing fresh gallons of milk down the drain as machinery got in a tangle. I was buffeted by hungry bullocks, chased by hissing geese, covered in slurry by rioting piglets and pecked unmercifully by spiteful hens sitting on eggs I was supposed to collect. I had nightmares about rats creeping out from dark hiding places at threshing time.

No room for sentimental twaddle, then, when blood-tingling action called as the binder coughed and spat out its sheaves. An army of village youngsters wielding sticks, some knobbly veterans of earlier campaigns and others freshly whittled on the way, charged on to the pastoral picture to give it a dramatic edge.

"There go one!" went up the cry. A startled rabbit had bolted from standing corn a few yards ahead of the binder. Panicked into utter confusion by shrieks of a chasing mob, it zig-zagged furiously before darting into the sanctuary of a clump of trees.

"There go another!" rose above the unbroken mechanical rhythms on the edge of this animated stage. Now a giant hare bounded perilously close to the tractor wheels, changed direction as if tugged back from danger by a piece of divine elastic and powered towards the wide ditch separating barley from sugar beet. My third harvest as a stick-waving son of the stubble, and nothing to show for all our running, roaring, sweating and threatening.

As we prepared to turn tail and review strategies for tomorrow or next summer, I spied a twitching movement next door to one of the rucksacks left on a tarpaulin used to cover the binder. At first I thought it was a dreaded rat looking for a free meal, but a second glance revealed a baby rabbit, shaking, cowering, pleading. The rest of the gang had nearly reached the gate as they urged me to get a move on if I wanted a bat before dusk. It was my turn to go in first.

I dropped my stick, moved gently towards the tiny ball of fur and coaxed it into action. It scampered over rucksack and tarpaulin and disappeared into a stubble jungle tall enough to offer instant security.

It was mighty hard to concentrate as our cricket match unfolded. I was bowled first ball. A blatant duck to go with my rabbit secret. I got over the urge to let the cat out of the rucksack by telling myself all the other harvest field marauders would have proved just as soft-hearted if those little eyes had blinked at them.

Coronation of the year with plenty of young subjects to join in the rural celebrations, be it chasing rabbits or helping to bring in the harvest.

Up in smoke

Old folk of the village still called the North Sea the German Ocean. A few years after the war, with our little community being welded back together in the middle of the county, that echo gave a faraway coastal world an air of mystery, almost a threatening touch as we sent up a customary prayer for fine weather.

The Sunday School seaside outing, with Hunstanton and Yarmouth vying for our excited custom, was one of the most eagerly-anticipated events on the calendar. Little brown envelopes flowed from superintendent Harry Dawson's waistcoat pocket as the green bus trundled past countless fields of golden stubble and singing started almost immediately to embarrass the only person concentrating on the road. "For he's a jolly good driver… " would earn a heartfelt reprise on the way home when Harry took up a collection in his cap.

For now, he was happy to reward regular youthful attendance on Sunday mornings at the Methodist Chapel. A full house of 52 or thereabouts brought precious shillings to go with savings rescued from fruit picking expeditions and harvest helping. Grown-ups unable to throw off the wartime cloak of austerity grimaced and grumbled as we contemplated the biggest spree of the year. Slot machines, donkey rides, candyfloss, roundabouts… such dreadful extravagances! No doubt venerable villagers suffered real pangs of guilt while tucking into mountains of fish and chips, cockles, whelks and jellied eels.

Hunstanton extended a homely welcome in the late 1940s when any trip out of the village was a big adventure. We looked in vain for the regal washing line as we passed the gates of Sandringham. Cheers rang out as we caught our first glimpse of the briny and those dramatic striped cliffs. I stayed close to the family circle after older boys offered to throw me fully-clothed into the water just to give post-war pollution a handy boost.

I could scoff at such threats by the time our seaside safari reached Yarmouth, bigger, brasher and much better suited to my determined search for an image. Perhaps it was only meant to last for a few hours, but I badly wanted to put a dent in that 'hick from the sticks' demeanour dogging me to grammar school. Now was the time to strike a few cool notes along the Golden Mile. Are you ready, world?

Tubby had been privy to some of my earlier seafront indiscretions. Like marching boldly to the top of the helter-skelter, discovering vertigo on peering across the sands and slinking meekly down all those steps to hand in my unused coconut mat. Shame compounded by a grinning attendant offering thrippence back for the worst impression of Sherpa Tenzing he had ever seen. Then there was the boating lake disaster culminating in the man on the microphone announcing with no hint of sympathy: "Come in number 6, your time is up – and so are the rescue flares". My efforts were hardly oar-inspiring, but there was no need to underline my landlubber pedigree in such a public manner.

Still, you have to go through choppy teenage waters to reach any fashionable port. Tubby, trusty first mate on scores of hazardous voyages, had every right to share my undiluted pleasure at sweeping ashore in the name of style, poise and growing confidence that country lads can soon learn which buttons to push.

I set the new straw hat at a jaunty angle, more eye-me-slow than kiss-me-quick, and snatched a few bars from the Crosby-Sinatra songbook. When The Blue Of The Night slid effortlessly into Violet For Your Furs as I warbled into an empty lemonade bottle and soaked up applause on a stage stretching from the Britannia Pier to the floral clock. I'd got them in the palm of my sweaty hand ready for the rousing finale.

I strolled nonchalantly from behind the tea-stall, my brand new pipe with curly stem packed with Three Nuns tobacco. All my savings had gone on these prize props in a bid for seaside stardom.

Lighting-up time outside the Winter Gardens. I winked at passing girls in between puffs, pants, coughs, spits, wheezes and strange little bouts of losing contact with sun swept reality. Tubby was holding my hat and pipe, thumping my back and asking if I had any last requests as a Golden Mile toilet swayed and swivelled like a mad refugee from the Pleasure Beach hold-tight department. Yes, I spluttered, keep this episode from everyone else on the bus and hide the pipe and tobacco at the bottom of my dinner bag. No, I didn't want pickle sandwiches and ginger beer right now. Thanks, but I could find the door on my own as soon as it came round again.

Sadly, that calamity by the side of the old German Ocean did not put me off smoking, although future pipe experiments were confined to rural hideaways where going green had nothing to do with growing appreciation of our natural environment. Impromptu outside concerts continued well into the skiffle and rock-and-roll era, but I managed to steer clear of dressing rooms with revolving doors, white enamel fittings and too many gurgling sounds.

Adventures on the coast...
slot machines, donkey rides, candyfloss, roundabouts...

Lords of harvest

Over the fields and far away. We could take a hint when jaded grown-ups peered at the calendar, sighed and decided long harvest holidays were meant to stretch legs, broaden minds and provide contributions towards new school outfits. Fruit-picking, corn-gathering and garden-tidying were orthodox means of reaping vital funds and keeping out of mischief most of the time. But the truly inventive, the genuinely ambitious foot soldiers in a rural army stationed on the headlands of adolescence sought less strenuous but more colourful and lucrative manoeuvres.

Thick sandwiches – we dubbed them doorsteps – and a bottle of cold tea or cocoa made up basic rations for dawn-to-dusk raids on foreign shores. Advance parties had pinpointed possible soft touches, like the retired shopkeeper, in a nearby parish, who really liked children and paid handsome fees for cleaning out her rabbits. Or the old smallholder with an endless number of jobs to be done involving sacks in a tumbledown barn. Very handy if it should happen to rain. Hopes could be cruelly dashed as reports came through of rabbits being sold or the barn being blown over by last week's storm. Now it was a case of probing the unknown, mustering enough resolve to turn down the first offer of instant employment in sure belief a true winner waited round the next corner.

We preferred to operate as a team, although few potential hirers seemed keen to take on three or four lads with more mardle than muscle. Mumbles about not concentrating properly or too many cooks trying the same menu signalled more hard decisions to be made – to go solo or stride on in the name of unyielding comrade-ship. On one momentous occasion, with the kitty at an embarrassing low and another day drifting nowhere, we landed what we considered to be the ultimate challenge to our co-operative spirit.

Our destination was three stubbled fields away, a matter of "well over one thousand acres" according to Tubby's questionable arithmetic as we blinked into an unrelenting sun. Our bikes were camouflaged among hemlock and hogweed at the back of a freshly-creosoted shed. Time for a healthy stroll into the heart of a captivating harvest scene that had tested us and found us seriously wanting, only a couple of weeks before on our home patch. However, this exercise had nothing to do with hard work showing up soft youngsters. Indeed, there was a fair chance the farmer and his bronzed troops would be delighted to see us, even if they did know we hailed from another village and had come a collective cropper in the Norfolk Agricultural Academy Entrance Exam (Level One, Harvest Hopefuls).

We had been entrusted with precious provisions for the afternoon break, commonly known as 'fourses' or 'wittles'. Not so much meals on wheels as snacks on the hoof. Perfectly straightforward, and sixpence each when we returned with empty tins, bags and jugs and inevitable praise for such tasty fare.

Tubby took charge of home-brewed beer supplies because he had the steadiest hand and would not be tempted to steal a sip or two. He had become a complete abstainer after an unfortunate incident involving partly-fermented blackberry wine and roll-up fags at an initiation ceremony organised by close friends the previous summer.

Ernie, who claimed such ceremonies were harmless if you didn't swallow or inhale, looked after shortcakes, sausage rolls and biscuits. He knew he would be tempted, but possessed the useful knack of shuffling things around so it didn't look as if any items had been removed let alone gorged in one go. He promised to obliterate all tell-tale crumbs as we reached the Promised Headland.

I was custodian of the rest – freshly-baked bread, big chunks of cheese, rosy apples and boiled sweets for that contemplative couple of minutes in the shade before work resumed.

Horses still ruled much of the farming kingdom when Keith Skipper and his chums were entrusted to take provisions across the stubbled acres. They couldn't resist a little light refreshment of their own along the way.

So we set forth, little Lords of the Harvest bearing gifts across the golden acres, our obeisance to the coronation of the year and time-tanned sons of the stubble bringing in the sheaves. It was thirsty work, so Tubby allowed us two gulps each from his biggest jug which could so easily have lurched out of control when we crossed the open ditch separating oats from barley. All that fresh air sharpened appetites as well, and our doorsteps, washed down with cold tea, had found welcome mats within minutes of leaving home that morning. We reckoned it was safe to lighten our late-afternoon load by three shortcakes, two sausage rolls, six biscuits, one apple and a selection of boiled sweets. We left the bread and cheese intact simply because it seemed a bit far-fetched to suggest famished rabbits, stoats and rats had set upon us and nibbled round the edges before guilt overcame them.

Our arrival was greeted with a mixture of delight and derision as the elevator fell silent and horses snorted approval at this break in routine. "We're bin a'waitin' for three strong boys to lend a hand. Dew yew send 'em this way if yew cum acrorst 'em on the way hoom!" chortled a man on top of a growing stack. He took off his cap and waved his pitchfork in mock salute.

Suddenly, we didn't feel quite so bad about helping ourselves. All we had done was land our blow first, an important lesson in the battle for survival among these masters of rural repartee. The farmer's wife increased our bounty to ninepence apiece when we passed on gratuitous compliments from her well-fed army. She was rather surprised at our refusal to select from shortcakes, sausage rolls, biscuits, apples and boiled sweets. She put it down to simple good manners as we retrieved bikes from the hemlock and hogweed jungle.

*If acorns abound in **September**,*

Snow will be deep in December.

September Saunters

Safely gathered in

I relish a few days of indolence in September, confident I can look back and forward at the same time. A habit fashioned out of youthful distaste for those who claimed it should not be done.

Teachers, parents and other bossy grown-ups invariably demanded a fresh approach after the harvest holidays. The start of a new school year meant turning over a new leaf, proving you could do better, realising all that exciting potential, putting bad habits behind one… good intentions crammed into a shiny new satchel alongside sharpened pencils and clean exercise books.

Just two lessons into that exciting new era and I was loafing down memory lane with a piece of chalk stinging one ear and a rasping reprimand bending the other. Working out the village cricket team averages pushed homework off the kitchen table as soon as latest confrontations with shiny conkers had been settled. Decimal points came alive as stirring cricket encounters with neighbouring parishes trotted out for another inspection.

Why should a sporting obsession go into hibernation just because the cows were back munching on the pitch? Did not that obsession play a vital role in my eventual appreciation of applied mathematics, local geography, human biology and proper joined-up writing? Grammar school teachers, with all their degrees and expertise in reading young minds, seemed sadly reluctant to recognise such bold embryonic efforts in the name of positive diversification.

Looking forward was an integral part of the exercise. I really wanted to be re-elected scorer and statistician at the annual meeting. The others had to fend for themselves amid dark rumours about pints changing hands with regard to certain players being tempted to move before the cattle were shooed away again from the sacred turf.

Now my modest playing days are over, I nod towards a host of cricket books waiting for winter digestion. Looking back and looking forward. September spells departures and arrivals, yesterdays and tomorrows, reflection and anticipation. Perhaps the mood is best caught by picking blackberries, when visions of cosy Sunday teas around the blazing hearth have to be tempered with acceptance of scratches, stings, bites, stains and cuts on the way.

I have been raiding Mother Nature's larder for well over 50 years, and she is still dishing out the same old rewards and reminders. The biggest and juiciest fruit are still a tantalising inch or two from your fingertips. A lesson for life to be lifted from a hedgerow. Torn trousers, plucked pullovers and real thorns in the side are predictable prices to pay for overblown ambition. And you still spot the plumpest clusters just waiting to fall into your basket while you are heading home. Not even my most respected teacher could tell me whose law that was.

September remains the heart of my favourite time of year, even though it does get late earlier. Green is still a fashionable country-side colour, but there are appealing alternatives. Hedges dripping red. Brown fields tend to shy away from the sun, but they are not yet ready for frost. Birds begin restless flights. Mornings turn cool and misty, urging you to make more of each day.

We watch the last holidaymakers melt away, wondering what new delights will lure them back next year. We know Santa Claus will be in the shops soon to stoke the commercial fires. We fear he could be rubbing beards with the Lord of the Harvest before long. For now, we hope our reflections will be allowed to play for a while, enjoying the late warmth, the haze of evening. September should never be rushed.

I recall bouts of harvest thanksgiving in chapel, church, school, rectory room and village hall that threatened to go on triumphantly until next year's crop was starting to flourish. Hymns of praise, sales of produce, community-binding suppers, barrels of ale, tales of the fields… how we loved the lingering over simple gratitude that yet again all was safely gathered in.

The village schoolteacher asked her infants to name some of the things they had seen at yesterday's harvest thanksgiving service.

"Carrots" said one child.

"Parsnips" answered another.

"Cabbages" called a third.

"Very good," replied the teacher. "Now can you give me one word to cover all these things?"

A long silence. Then a little lad, a son of a son of the soil, put up his hand.

"Please, Miss," he piped, "Gravy."

Time for one last swing on the gate before a new school year beckoned and youngsters packed their satchels.

Now, that answer showed rare powers of invention and originality, a memorable line from September's song before autumn's shawl started slipping over summer's final hours. But he was probably told he could do better.

Licensed to shrill

Despite the first embarrassing rash of adolescent acne, I was flattered to be dubbed Lesser-Spotted Rustic Warbler by an old farm worker. He tuned in regularly as I sped past on my bike, lifting his head from concentration on the good earth to shake it in disbelief at a bad impression of Guy Mitchell, David Whitfield or Ronnie Ronalde.

I had a varied menu, song and tunes interspersed with cricket commentary from John Arlott at Lord's as Compton and Edrich put the Aussies to flight before lunch. Crowd noises crackled across the headlands as bats were raised in triumph and my clenched fist saluted another England success. On a good morning I could manage the opening strains of Music While You Work, Family Favourites and Paul Temple. Never mind these boy bands chasing up and down the pop charts of today... how about one lad on his own providing an all-round entertainment service as he pedalled along yesterday's lanes!

On my village round of Saturday morning errands, Ronnie Ronalde was the role model of the wireless accumulator age. His million-selling record If I Were A Blackbird inspired thousands like me to puff, purse and preen in the hope of producing a clear, piercing blast designed to turn heads and worry cats.

Whistling went automatically with whittling, walking or riding a bike. Some of my mates hissed through teeth or fingers until a crystal shaft of sound alerted the parish that another performer was licensed to shrill. I never mastered that art. Ronnie also showed outstanding singing and yodelling talents on his Sunday wireless programme, and only Donald Peers and Dick Barton came close to matching his adulation marks in our country household.

When I yodelled on my way to chop kindling, wash eggs, tidy gardens and keep the copper up the corner boiling, worried residents were known to leave their kitchens hastily to express sincere hopes that I had not injured myself too badly when my foot slipped and got caught in the chain. Neighbourhood Watch was a much more intimate concern in those days.

A chance to brush up my falsetto efforts came with the arrival of three Irishmen next door. They brought with them a wind-up gramophone and a record of Slim Whitman singing China Doll. They played it countless times before going to work on the farm, and, just in case you missed the dawn chorus, they wore out another needle before and after much-needed evening refreshment breaks in the village pub. We were awash in wavering warbles, and Mother led a chorus of relief when our musical neighbours invested in a good old-fashioned rendering of When Irish Eyes Are Smiling.

Norfolk audiences were surprisingly receptive as I took my burgeoning talents on the road. Parking my bike in the nearest ditch, I found a lucrative platform among the concrete mixers and piles of bricks on the site where new council houses were emerging just past the chapel. The workers were starved of live entertainment, and I could spare a few minutes between Saturday morning chores.

I mixed it up carefully, a sacred solo here from the Sunday School anniversary programme and a hip-swivelling number there from the popular charts heard under the bedclothes on come-and-go Radio Luxembourg. A few verses dredged up from a Victorian collection designed to melt the hardest of hearts – blind beggar boys with cherubic smiles converting vile workhouse masters into caring souls – provided a perfect finale. The hat went round as a well-nourished army of builders counted their blessings and gave thanks with their pennies.

Tubby, with just a hint of envy as I bought two packets of sweet cigarettes instead of the customary one, suggested the men were using that retiring collection to get rid of me rather than as a token of their appreciation. I challenged him to clamber on to a wobbly plank-stage supported by a pair of oil-drums and unashamed self-confidence to put on his own show. He pleaded a mixture of natural modesty and sheer panic at the very thought of such a performance. In any case, he was busy on Saturday mornings helping to muck out his father's pigs.

Entertainment on the move was quite common. We had a postman who could whistle in time with his pedalling, while several locals betrayed their imminent approach with a familiar hum or ditty. Delivery men had special signature tunes; The Old Rugged Cross accompanied one batch of groceries and The Dambusters March heralded a change of accumulator. The Corona Man naturally wanted to be top of the pops, and so his presentation did alter regularly. Unfortunately, a distinctly mournful voice took the edge off the brightest of numbers and they finished up sounding all the same. Now, if he could have picked up a round in Tin Pan Alley...

Perhaps the zenith of my whistle-and-ride career was to feature in an unlikely duet one Sunday afternoon as I dawdled along Dairy Drift and then turned towards the Rectory. The combination of day and location may have inspired my choice of offering, When The Lord Comes To Gather His Jewels. My version was more Hank Williams than Church Fellowship, much more wandering cowboy than visiting preacher. But it struck a chord with an unseen admirer on the other side of a tall hawthorn hedge. The voice joined in the chorus. A loud wolf-whistle and hosanna greeted the end of the number.

"Capital show! I don't know whether to take up a silver collection or bring choir practice forward... " The parson recognised raw talent in the saddle when he heard it.

Hark and ride... life's rich cycle in the countryside encouraged plenty of whistling and singing when pedal power ruled the roads.

Swaffham safaris

As I sit totting up the years and contemplating my novel waiting so patiently to be born, it suddenly dawns on me how significant September has been along life's enchanting Norfolk pathway. No wonder it's my favourite month as nights pull in and memories stretch out to warm them.

I graduated from village classroom to grammar school on a mixture of bicycle power and railway steam in September, 1955. The Pedlar of Swaffham was waiting to remind me how rich treasure could be unearthed by those prepared to dig deep under the tree of knowledge. It took me about 15 terms to find a spade.

I transported joined-up writing skills to Thetford in September, 1962, to start my career as Beeston's first overspill contribution to the town's journalistic ranks. Tom Paine was waiting to alert me to the dangers of inflammatory language. It took me about 15 lines to upset local footballers.

I exchanged quill for microphone in September, 1980, when the BBC showed commendable sense in extending its local wireless network into Norfolk. Terry Wogan was waiting to show how ridiculously easy this broadcasting business could be. It took me about 15 years to discover he might have been kidding.

September watersheds or, as an old Norfolk farm worker put it in his colourful vernacular, "jumpin' over hidges when yew dunt know woss on th'uther side". Perhaps I didn't leap into the unknown so much as stumble into it, but he was surprisingly perceptive for someone who treated a trip to the next village as an adventure of epic proportions.

Safaris to Swaffham and back immediately tested my raw credentials as a traveller clutching satchel, season ticket and sincere hopes I wouldn't be asked to reveal a passport on entering the grammar school gates. It was with considerable relief I noticed plenty of other hesitant newcomers from Cowmuck-and-Sugarbeetland. We stuck together in those early days, glorying in our country roots while town boys tried to swank their way to the front of the class with stories of marvellous leisure and sporting facilities, fathers in posh office jobs and an embarrassment of riches when it came to nubile maidens impressed by a smart uniform of yellow and black. We countered with gripping yarns of survival beyond the A47 in a world without electricity, mains sewerage, traffic congestion or trivial chat about the previous evening's television offerings. A regular shortage of nubile maidens simply meant we were more selective than town Romeos spoilt for choice.

We did have steam radio, and so we could join in the great media debate of September, 1955, even if our views tended to be one-sided. As ITV went on the air, the good old BBC hit back with a dramatic wireless winner. Grace Archer, one of the leading characters in the everyday story of countryfolk from Ambridge, died in a fire. "Just a coincidence" smirked the BBC as their new commercial rivals complained of a deliberate plot to steal their opening thunder. The ratings war had started in earnest, and I soon had reason to detest the growing influence of that flickering box up the corner. There was a chimp called Skipper in, I think, a cultural American import called Beverly Hillbillies. There was a blasted bush kangaroo chris-tened Skippy in one of those memorable Australian programmes where animals looked far more at home in front of the cameras than humans. Skippy had his own little theme song which haunts me to this day. I often thought of ending it all in the billabong nearest to Fransham railway station.

However, there were consolations to keep me going. "Let's have our Skipper batting last and fielding in front of the biology lab. Ho, ho, ho!" Old joke, but a fresh sense of belonging each time I wasn't left to act as the waste paper basket at the other end. Come to think of it, that must have been around the time when 'Rubbish Skip' jibes started. My masters were slightly more sophisticated in their name-calling, and I suppose it all helped to fashion a sense of humour when clouds of ignorance and uncertainly rolled my way.

Another milestone as
Keith chats to wireless wizard
Terry Wogan at the opening
of BBC Radio Norfolk in 1980.

"Capitaine!". Mr Chick, the French master, beamed as he boomed it out. I didn't know my acute from my grave, and the accent was on drawing attention to one of mid-Norfolk's lesser lights in the languages department. Mr Bowle, my chemistry master, picked up the theme as he dubbed me 'Cabin Boy', a position befitting someone who couldn't tell his acid from his alkaline. I fared little better in the woodwork room where the legendary Harry Carter amused himself and frightened the boys by shouting out "Scupper!" when my chisel slipped and the dovetail fanned into disaster. Then biology lessons came to a raucous halt when some bright spark mentioned there were butterflies called Skippers. There was a Large Skipper, a Small Skipper, the Essex Skipper and – cue howls of derision – the Dingy Skipper. I wanted to take wing and seek out another billabong.

Perhaps the most important lesson to emerge from those September hours of 1955 was the discovery that there is always someone worse off than yourself. A lad called Cocker had to endure constant baiting along these memorable lines often shared by two of his closest friends:

"Did you know Cocker's brother is a parrot?"

"No, how do you work that one out?"

"Well, he's a Cocker too!"

Schoolboy humour scarcely worth a mark of eleven-plus out of a hundred – but it had 'em rolling in the aisles. I even saw the teachers tittering.

*Ice in **October** to bear a duck,*

Nothing afterwards but slush and muck.

October Oddities

Ghosts on the runway

We had the perfect adventure playground, the envy of neighbouring villages. Keeping out marauders was a full-time job as darkness fell so soon after tea. The old aerodrome fairly crackled with ghostly sounds throughout the network of crumbling huts and musty tunnels.

A measure of salvation dwelt around the friendly Nissen hut that served as village hall. Our stocks of courage replenished, we exchanged bikes for Hurricanes and Spitfires. Down the runway, arms akimbo, hobnailed boots sparking and lips trembling with strange noises.

That should have been enough to scare off any aliens. Then again, such peculiar antics might well have attracted them through the twilight, down the weed-crusted drifts and past the wall with a painting, peeling rapidly, of a plane and a pretty young woman wearing little more than a smile. Some said she was a goddess sent to look after young airmen stationed here just over a decade before. One elder at the Chapel said she was a hussy bent on the Devil's work. We thought she brightened the place up.

These aliens seemed none too interested in an open-air art gallery or delicate matters of morality. They had come from next-door Litcham with a challenge – and we would accept it without question if we knew what was good for us. A convincing argument as they prowled and glared by swanky steeds decked out in new dynamos, shiny mudguards and pumps with proper connections. There were six of them and four of us. They were taller, wider, louder and could sneer better by miles. Although we were on our own midden and could probably out-talk them, it seemed sensible to curtail this confrontation at dusk by agreeing to their terms.

An October sporting showdown was to be staged on Litcham Common two Saturdays hence. Conkers, wrestling, a very rough version of leap-frog called 'ribcrusher' and bike-racing were the main events. Marbles would come into it if a smooth patch could be found. Ultimatums had already been delivered to Mileham Maulers and Tittleshall Troshers... roll up and get a legitimate good hiding or stay away and risk a really nasty invasion after dark.

As usual, the dice were loaded heavily in favour of Litcham Louts – that was our name for them as opposed to the official label of Liberators – and a hasty council-of-war was convened to settle on tactics for this rustic mini-Olympics. It was agreed unanimously to concentrate on conkers.

Ernie had strung countless victories together without resorting (as far as we knew) to soaking in vinegar or baking in the oven. He simply selected the best, dark mahogany, polished and shining, factory-fresh from the workshop of the trees, and knew instinctively that most of the bigger ones were lily-livered. Just like boys in other parishes when confronted by sheer class. Ernie was our main hope for points and a little bit of pride. Beeston Braves would not be humiliated!

That left Tubby to look after wrestling, Rodney to sample the delights of 'ribcrusher' and me to make a mark at bike-racing. I also stood by for marbles because I hadn't lost mine. (I said as much without knowing why it might be funny)

Our training stints intensified. Ernie was quietly confident as he gleaned beneath the trees. The rest of us grappled, jumped, pedalled and rolled with a fatalistic sort of air. On the Wednesday before sporting combat, as the pretty young woman wearing little more than a smile looked down benignly on a new breed of would-be heroes, we suffered a cruel blow.

Ernie went home feeling unwell. Next day he was confined to quarters with chickenpox. We kept going round for hourly bulletins in the hope it was wildly contagious. No way we could head for Litcham Common without our star performer.

Word came through of a virulent outbreak of cowardice in Mileham and a rash of new Saturday jobs in Tittleshall. A familiar whiff of triumphalism slipped out of Litcham in the shape of a message from the baker's roundsman that the sporting extravaganza had been cancelled. Our charming hosts didn't fancy having a go at each other.

Although we breathed a collective sigh of relief, and gave thanks to the aerodrome goddess for keeping us clear of the runway to calamity, we couldn't help wondering if a defining moment in village rivalry had not gone begging.

Surely Ernie, our all-conkering champion, would have knocked spots off the rest. He didn't pass on his chickenpox. So we avoided infection and the Litcham mini-Olympics – with no strings attached.

A boisterous version of leap-frog in the playground… concentration and timing are key ingredients for success.

Friendly monsters

My notoriety as one of Norfolk's leading non-drivers may have its roots in mechanical misadventures of nearly 50 years ago.

There was time and space then to collect registration numbers as vehicles trundled through the village, a steady trickle broken only by the occasional full-throttle flood of a newcomer to the motor-bike ranks eager to impress. I was alarmed when my oldest brother obtained one of these mighty monsters, but simply could not lose face in front of all my mates when he invited me to go for a test spin along the wide-open miles of the old aerodrome.

As pillion passengers go, I was rather relieved to come back. A vow never to repeat the grisly exercise remains unbroken to this day after a useful impression of living rigor mortis. I just could not yield to corners and sway with man and machine, clinging desperately to a basic belief that a bolt upright approach represented the only slim chance of going home and being recognised by the rest of the family. Wet through with sweat, rigid with fear and deaf to the sort of half-mocking applause gladiators used to get if they survived to fight another round, I left the runway rabble for a quiet lane where I could exorcise a few traumas with a good shake and sob. This sort of breakdown warranted no pick-up truck.

When my brother came a cropper a couple of weeks later and broke his leg, I knew it was my destiny to avoid all future contact with these dastardly macho-machines. I took that bit of catching cardboard out of the spokes of the back wheel of my bicycle to avoid any connections with those who made noises about joining the high-speed set as soon as possible. I even refused to show obvious signs of remorse when the contraption we put together in Tubby's orchard came to an undignified halt and crumbled two yards out of the starting blocks for our soapbox derby against the tearaways of Litcham. No, speed did not impress me. And should it be allied to a thunderous racket, all the more reason to shun it.

Perhaps this was a legacy of the agricultural era into which I threw myself – and missed – just after the last war. Majestic horses still attracted plenty of subjects, even if they no longer ruled the furrows with impunity. The switch from Suffolk Punch to Fordson Major had to be a painful one for any rookie in the farmyard army who insisted on shouting "Whooooa!" instead of utilising clutch and brake. When deep misgivings mounted alongside insults flying my way, I kept wondering how time-tanned suns of the stubble had coped with the revolution from swinging scythe to clicking binder. Bringing in the sheaves was meant to be an archaic rite rather than a mechanical process...

Soon binders would be pushed aside completely by combines, real monsters going against the grain, doing away with sheaf, stook and rick. No work for thatchers or threshers. The centuries-old tradition of gathering up the year's work taken away from the labourers by one all-powerful bully. Romance by the acre, maybe, but I had to find some reasonable excuse for being born a bit later than inner-most feelings allowed. As I read more country writers, it became clear I was in good company. Even those who could handle the physical demands, as well as dramatic advances in countryside technology, admitted freely that increased efficiency invariably made the farm a duller, quieter, lonelier place.

Let me slip in another little confession here. I mustered a measure of grudging admiration for some monsters on my boyhood scene, albeit from a safe distance. Steam engines did make a lot of noise, but they moved at a stately pace and generated awesome power. They were undoubted kings of threshing time, throbbing steadily and rocking slightly forwards and backwards while countless wheels and belts criss-crossed and twirled on either side of the shaking drum. The oily smell of the engine, the musty tang of the straw, a mushroom of black smoke billowing above a frantic canvas... A good day's troshin' coated in dust and chaff brought out hordes of spectators to watch a well-organised team in action.

A steamroller crunched by occasionally, usually on a road-mending mission, gorging itself on a menu of tar and chippings. The first months of my grammar school career were marked by steam train travel between Fransham and Swaffham. I am glad to have caught a genuine whiff of an era re-created regularly nowadays, especially for tourists and new recruits to the rural campaign for capturing authentic sounds and smells from the past.

However, I nursed no ambitions to be an engine driver on road, rail or down on the farm with the troshin' troops. I was much safer leading a horse than revving up a tractor. I feel no guilt at being a mechanical failure as Norfolk's highways now demand more care and attention than many can give.

That nightmare ride on the back of my brother's motorbike did me a power of good in a funny sort of way. Well, it told me to slow down and keep my feet on the ground. Sensible advice for a Norfolk lad on the highroad to self-discovery.

Steam engines were friendly monsters on the Norfolk scene, moving at a stately pace and generating awesome power.

Tour de Norfolk

We had heard of the Tour de France, a bicycle race of many stages with a yellow jersey for the overall leader. Ernie, most sartorially-minded of our village clan, wondered how you could ride hundreds of miles in jersey and overalls. I told him it all depended on the size of your handlebar moustache, while Tubby chipped in with his favourite uncle's definition of the Norfolk three-speed model – "slow, dead slow and backwards!"

Our bike banter intensified as we became more dependent upon our machines, first to get to school way beyond familiar home boundaries and then for exciting weekend expeditions into new territory. October's sun was warm and inviting enough to put a genuine missionary zeal into plans for our version of the Tour de Norfolk. Well, just a small slice of the county, and that as far as possible from horrible main roads, but it still represented an awesome challenge for country lads who had not long been intro- duced to pedals, pumps and punctures.

For much of the first decade of our lives we relied solely on our legs to get about, a pertinent point worth passing on to the current gener- ation of car-cocooned youngsters. The bike was a truly liberating influence for those seeking signs of life past the old stone quarry, the churchyard a fair distance from the village and the runway where young Americans had taken off in B24 Liberators for combat missions only a dozen or so years earlier. Not that history, geography and their deeply significant impact on the social climate in which we were being raised headed our list of priorities. We were more interested in conkers, nuts you could eat, prime clusters of blackberries, tumble-down barns full of straw and adventures waiting to happen and ponds where we could resume ducks and drakes rivalry, making flat stones skip along the water like bouncing bombs destroying German dams. The war still fed our imaginations.

We made countless pit stops on that first journey of discovery, treating every new stretch of water like some mighty ocean asking to be charted. The first rich, musty smells of autumn and bands of gold, red and brown wheeling round fields, trees and hedges reminded us this was Norfolk putting on one of its most spectacular shows. Without really knowing it, we were soaking up nature's bounty, sharing timeless seasonal glories, storing away images and experiences destined to line years to come against cynicism and too much regret. "Nice out here, ent it?" was Tubby's concession to finer feelings. "Any sandwiches left?" was Ernie's predictable counter to the prospect of a soppy interlude before we returned to the saddle.

Mileham won our inaugural vote for most hospitable place on our pedalling rounds. Hardly a surprise, really, as Tubby's Nan and Gran both lived there and the shop produced wonderful home-made lollipops in the shape of egg-cups. Even so, I was staggered to discover at the end of October, 1992, that Mileham had been singled out for the title of worst village in the country for accepting newcomers.

A survey, blatantly designed to raise Norfolk blood pressures along with a posh magazine's circulation, considered only a small sample of parishes across the United Kingdom, and the researcher admitted she had not spoken to any Suffolk or Cambridgeshire residents. Nor was it made clear how the whole silly business had been conducted among Norfolk natives and newcomers. After all, it is important what you ask, how you ask it and who is invited to give answers.

It added up to the same old story of confusing caution with coldness and pride with prejudice. Why, even in the good old 1950s we had to tread carefully up the path to free refreshments – and we travelled all of two miles!

Litcham, Tittleshall, Longham, Bittering, Wendling, the Franshams, the Dunhams, the Lexhams, Beetley, North Elmham… they fell like ninepins to our growing appetite for travel. Some calls revived painful memories of too much graft in the recent summer sun, picking beans at Gorgate, near Gressenhall, and harvesting black-currants at Little Fransham and Whissonsett for example, but now these were more leisurely encounters along the mid-Norfolk trail.

Just occasionally, and mainly to avoid the threat of grim chores on our own patch, we would strike out on trips patently beyond our capabilities. I recall an ill-fated attempt to reach Swaffham before noon on a Saturday, only to spy the outskirts of Necton at teatime and decide to scurry for home before complete darkness swallowed us up. We badly wanted to sample the delights of Castle Acre one Sunday after a boy at school told me a girl who lived there was sweet on me. She had two good-looking friends. Working on the assumption they would probably have invited a Beeston biking trio to get lost, we did… somewhere near Colkirk.

Minor diversions on our memorable Tour de Norfolk when roads were safer and quieter, ambitions less than grandiose and every village had its own distinctive flavour. We introduced ourselves to many out of simple curiosity. We went home assured a host of signposts would point to lasting friendships.

If you wed in bleak
November,

Only joy will come,
remember.

November Notions

Matchless moments

The preacher seemed to be looking straight at me as he hammered out his text: "Men loved darkness rather than light, because their deeds were evil!" How on earth did he know about our plans to liven up a few of the village's grumpiest characters? And was it really that bad to use a traditional celebration to score a point or two in the 1950s generation game?

Bonfire and brimstone enveloped the Chapel pulpit that Sunday night. I feared my eyebrows would be singed and my soul condemned to eternal damnation. As if to reinforce a pall of guilt swirling over my head, the old tortoiseshell stove started to spit out barbs of acrid smoke. I snatched a grain of consolation from the preacher's fiery repetition of his text to conclude the sermon: "Men loved darkness…" Ah, he had grown-ups in mind rather than young lads with a puckish streak. Gunpowder, treason and plot could hardly be classed as deadly sins when unravelled on such a parochial stage.

Thunderclaps of a new rural theology kept me company on the way home. "Blessed are the noisemakers, for they shall teach old miseries a lesson… Love thy neighbour as thyself, unless he or she happens to be totally beyond a joke… Remember ye the eleventh commandment – thou shalt not get caught!"

I met a man with a fizzing tilley-lamp. He was off to attend to calves beyond the dairy. "Night, boy, an' dunt be leart in the mornin'. Bring yer hoe cors we're gorn muckspreddin'!" He chortled at his homespun wit and disappeared from view. At least he was safe from our purge of ill-tempered personalities.

The Monday night moon played hide-and-seek with heavy clouds as we moved stealthily along the drift. Tubby had the old tin can. Ernie was in charge of our precious Little Demon and matches. I organised the safest route to Crikey's back door past a clutter of empty rabbit hutches, broken pallets and rusty bedsteads. And a rogue bicycle wheel with loose spokes playing crazy roulette with my left leg and a broom handle as navigation skills foundered at the vital time. I yelped instructions to retreat. The bicycle wheel came with us as far as the hedge. A door creaked open but we didn't hang about for any exchange of November pleasantries.

Tuesday night's drizzle carried an icy edge as we embarked on another ill-fated safari, this time towards the newer council houses just past the Chapel. The woman who helped with school dinners, but extended her curriculum to dealing swiftly with boys possessing a strange sense of humour, was our intended target. She never received our calling card on the doorstep because Ernie had allowed the matches to get damp. The woman's husband, tall and menacing, emerged from a garden shed. He must have sensed that our furtive presence had little to do with inquiries about semolina on tomorrow's menu. We melted into the darkness, Little Demon intact.

A hasty meeting of the travelling pyrotechnics display team behind the bike shed next day voted in favour of the ultimate challenge, taking a big bang to serenade the old farmer who had chased us from his cart shed the summer before last after weeks of work to turn it into a comfortable new gang headquarters. He lived on the very edge of the parish, down a long lane full of potholes and past the deserted stone pit.

They said the pit was haunted, although a photograph unearthed for a church exhibition of local memories showed a trio of turn-of-the-century workers at ease in their surroundings. We took a degree of comfort from their posed cheerfulness as the third and final leg of our great nocturnal adventure beckoned. Three likely lads of the modern era, full of enterprise and determination, we didn't need pick, rake and shovel to make a mark in the country-side. Just a tin can, Little Demon and dry matches...

"Have you got them, Tubby?" A worried shake of the head. Ernie gazed at me, willing a positive reply out of a growing climate of juvenile fear and concern. No, my job was navigation, and as far as I could tell we were about to pass the old stone pit.

Matchless moments of undiluted terror raced in to replace our name-calling antics. A man with a fizzing tilley-lamp suddenly grew out of the bushes. We didn't bother to ask if he had any dry matches on him. He urged us not to be late in the morning and to bring our hoes for muckspreading purposes. Well, that's what it sounded like as we turned and scarpered and panted and stumbled over the potholes like Jumping Jacks out of control.

We didn't venture out again after dark until Bonfire Night itself. Then the Little Demon burst its lungs as Tubby dropped it into the tin can and Ernie proudly brandished a new box of matches. A satis-fying moment to some extent, but it tended to lose something out there in the open, well away from the dangerous worlds of Crikey's back yard, the dinner lady's doorstep and the old stone pit with its ghosts, real and imaginary.

Stone pit workers at the turn of the century stand to attention for the photographer. This scene played its part in the nocturnal adventures of Keith Skipper and his village pals as they plotted a firework treat down a long lane full of potholes in the early 1950s.

Beyond the pail

I fought so hard to remain faithful to my home patch during those growing-up years when it was easy to make eyes at bigger and brasher corners of the Norfolk empire. Our little world, soaked in farming ways and simple tastes, chugged along gently well away from the main roads and a good seven miles from the nearest flesh-pots tempting and tantalising a post-war generation in Dereham.

Not so much a case of limited horizons as gratitude for an unash-amedly old-fashioned country community in which to blossom as a polite, thoughtful, healthy, intelligent and sensitive lad. Well, that's how I saw and felt it before falling foul of the deadly sin of envy. All of a sudden, insecurity, dissatisfaction and resentment accom-panied my bike rides beyond the parish boundaries.

We had learned to live with Litcham dependence. Our larger neigh-bour just up the road provided many necessities, doctor, policeman, baker and bus service among them. They had more pubs and shops and one of the strongest football teams in the area. Whenever I boasted how Beeston produced the mighty Jem Mace, father of modern scientific boxing, Litcham punched back with a flurry of blows from the past. We could not match a thriving market, a tanning industry, a cock-pit, a racecourse, a fire brigade, village stocks and a local concert party called The Litcham Mirthquakes.

We were learning to accept Litcham's superiority, even if we did have the temerity to test it now and again with an invasion inspired by Mace's world-conquering exploits. Litcham Common was the appointed arena. Verbal sparring echoes across the gorse, bramble and heath. Impromptu scuffles sent birds and rabbits scurrying. We usually settled for a tactical retreat, pedalling furiously as shame chased us all the way home.

All these comparisons and incidents paled into nothing, however, alongside the green-eyed monster waiting to hitch a ride round the streets of Litcham. We simply could not contain our jealousy of their carriage of convenience and the colourful character in charge of it. Let me set the scene with a potent extract from The Short History of a Mid-Norfolk Village by Dr Eric Puddy, first published in 1957 and recently given a deserved second innings by Litcham Historical Society:

"At the appointed times, the night soil cart could be heard rumbling up the street, lit by an old-fashioned candle-lantern swinging from the outside shaft. The rumbling of the wheels would cease, and within seconds arose the snoring of Wally Feeke's old mule. Pails clanked, the midnight air became less ambient, the mule woke with a start and moved along to the next cottage as in a fantasy."

Can there be any wonder that Wally and his honeycart should drive such deep stakes of envy into the hearts of boys from just over the border? With no prospect of Beeston setting up a rival service, we knew instinctively that one of the key chapters in local social history was being played out – and all we could do was stand and admire. It didn't help when fresh stirring escapades were added to a growing legend. Wally lived with danger. It was inherent in his calling. It really started that night in wartime when his honeycart was hijacked...

He was busy patrolling Back Street. While he was away from the cart for a couple of minutes, two American servicemen (stationed at Beeston, I'm ashamed to report) jumped on his chariot and charged up the Lexham Road at full gallop. An hour later they returned with more than a whiff of scandal. They had travelled at such a rate that the movement of the cart's contents had forced open the lid. The hijackers were soaked.

Wally Feeke and his honeycart, the cause of deep envy among boys in the village next door. A framed copy of this picture by Peter Rowe, was presented to Keith Skipper by Litcham Historical Society.

Wally did not bother to ring up the White House after an adventure designed to stretch USA-Litcham relations to the limit. He simply scowled: "That'll larn them bludder Yanks!"

Perhaps Wally's most telling pronouncement as to how every job carries its perks came with Friday night calls at Lenny Allison's local fish and chip shop. A packed house parted like the Red Sea as Wally walked in. He never once had to wait for his piece and six. Many were tempted to ask if he'd get theirs while he was there.

In snowy weather, the only way he could make progress was to place sacks in front of the horse and cart. Expeditions took twice as long, and there were times when he got days behind the calls of nature. Wally hated bad weather, but he would not shirk a challenge. Another reason why his band of ardent admirers continued to grow. So there were many good yarns coming out of Litcham with Wally's exploits assuming heroic proportions. Delivery men making tracks to our cottage door brought a new story, or a neatly embellished one, from Wally's latest rounds – a one-man soap opera with enough thrilling instalments to keep a clutch of mid-Norfolk villages hooked for a long time.

Eventually, envy had to give way to unstinting admiration. To some degree, Wally's career fired an abiding interest in village life and lore. One of my proudest possessions is a framed picture of the Litcham legend getting on with a job that had so many others turning up their noses. It was presented to me by Wally's widow May, on behalf of Litcham Historical Society.

As an honorary member of that hard-working organisation, I am kept in touch with what goes on in the village today as well as enjoying regular jaunts beyond the pail and Wally's memorable trail.

A real privilege for a boy from just over the border.

Football fever

Perhaps the seeds were sown among the cowpats and comic cavortings of a grim Saturday in November when it was deemed reasonable for touchline experts to huddle together for warmth.

I was small enough to hide inside the army coat of our largest and loudest supporter as he stamped his feet, spat on his hands, banged them together and blasted anyone who couldn't follow simple instructions. He blew my emergency cover twice as his nippy nephew raced clear of defenders and had only the goalkeeper to beat. Twice a substance left behind by a member of the banished dairy herd put skids under glory hopes, and the ball ended up way beyond the old shepherd's hut on wheels used as a dressing room.

Ah, the theatre of Mid-Norfolk life! Ambitions dashed, loyalties tested, plots thickening, heroes and villains multiplying, bit-part players stepping into the spotlight... such compelling entertainment on the village stage. I was getting used to the wonderful vagaries of cricket as scorer and statistician under blissful skies. Now, seeking refuge from an icy wind snaking across the old aerodrome, I began to appreciate the cut-and-thrust and disparate thrills of the great winter game.

Coagulated cowpats, comic capers, caustic comments – vital ingredients on the Saturday afternoon menu for any budding sports reporter. Certainly they came in handy when I realised it might be easier to write about mortal combat rather than try it for myself.

Suspicions on that score were harshly confirmed in my first term at grammar school when I talked my way into the under-13s team to take on Gaywood Park of King's Lynn. They were bigger, stronger and faster, well worth their victory by an embarrassing margin. I played wide on the right. Well, that's a bit of an exaggeration. I ran up and down forlornly a few times, usually without ball or hope, and came to a tacit agreement with a snorting, sneering, muscle-loaded full-back that I'd keep out of his way if he promised not to kick me. It worked a treat. He lorded it over our side of the pitch, set up at least four goals with totally unhindered runs and thanked me cordially at the end for having the good sense to co-operate.

I discovered a surprising turn of speed at the final whistle to avoid an instant inquest into such abject surrender. I never played for the school again, and only turned out in a house match four years later because the captain had a strange sense of humour. He wanted to boost interest by including performers guaranteed to reduce the opposition to helpless laughter. "We'll strike while they're holding their sides," he suggested in a team talk that seemed rather short on genuine tactical awareness. We raised a few chuckles, and did cause a spot of confusion by stopping dead to call for oxygen on the one occasion when we broke through. But a16-0 scoreline hinted at the need for a bit of tightening up in the search for funnybones. After all, our opponents tended to ease up in the final 70 minutes.

Remarkably, I maintained strong interest in football, attending village home fixtures in all weathers, cheering on family and friends even when odds and goals were stacked against them. I could 'read' the game even if I couldn't play it with any degree of confidence, and my impromptu commentaries, inspired by fast-talking Raymond Glendenning on the wireless, became regular features on the Beeston scene.

A couple of referees cautioned me to keep quiet, although they couldn't explain which rule I was supposed to be breaking. A visiting goalkeeper ordered me to stay away from the area behind his net after he'd let in three soft goals and earned the description of "a lumbering liability who couldn't catch a bus if it pulled up and parked outside his house".

My big break as a soccer pundit arrived with a spying mission to Litcham Common. The village next door boasted a top-notch team, the envy of rival players, officials and supporters for miles around.

Their supremacy was bound to rankle most among closest neighbours, and my task, fortified by a quarter of pear drops purchased by those who sent me, involved close scrutiny of personnel and methods. I ignored catcalls from the youthful home followers long conditioned to making life uncomfortable for interlopers from Beeston, flashed my new notebook, licked my pencil and prepared to compile the most revealing dossier in the history of local sporting rivalry. The exercise lasted just under eight minutes.

Deep deliberations on the halfway line were rudely interrupted by a beefy boot into touch from a desperate defender. I didn't see the ball coming – not the first time I was to pay for having my nose deep into a book – and I crumpled to the turf with the leather ball manufacturer's name clearly imprinted on a tear-stained face. A kind man with a small lorry returned me to the bosom of my family, lifting my prostrate form from the back like a butcher delivering meat. Mild concussion confined me to bed for the rest of the weekend, recovery scarcely aided by Tubby and Ernie calling to inquire if it was a left hook or a right uppercut responsible for my sad condition.

When I embarked on a 25-year professional career of sports reporting, with football fixtures stretching from village green to Wembley, I vowed to be kind to below-average performers full of good intentions – and to always keep a careful eye on the ball.

Double delight… Beeston footballers and officials on parade with the North Norfolk Cup and Necton Shield at the end of their successful 1947-48 season.

Have you seen God's Christmas tree in the sky,

With its trillions of tapers blazing high?

December Delights

Cowshed carols

The most demanding village expedition of the year beckoned. We wrapped up carefully and turned up cheerfully outside the Chapel straight after tea. As a keen wind probed and threatened darker mischief later on, we warmed ourselves on thoughts of the annual Sunday School party among the pews.

Harry's hurricane lamp, on a rare outing, seemed to have a mind of its own, hissing and swinging on the end of a pole. Bertha's accordion was soon pulling her along, opening notes punching holes in the country darkness. Although the instrument would have been more at home in a pub singalong, it did serve us better than Walter's ancient violin. He had tried to start us from scratch on three previous occasions, and was encouraged to take a rest when his musical efforts roused every dog in the neighbourhood to form a rival choir. Bertha borrowed the accordion because she accepted a harmonium on wheels was not a practical alternative to a keen but uninspiring fiddler on the hoof.

Veterans of these carol-singing marathons knew the importance of conserving energy and enthusiasm. Just a couple of verses from Away In A Manger for families with children at the council houses. An abridged version of As With Gladness Men Of Old before eight o'clock for Auntie May in The Street. Anything short and fairly melodic for Walter as he hauled back the curtains and recalled contributions of other years.

We had to present a united and unflagging front on arrival at The Major's large residence, simply because a good performance would earn much-needed refreshments along with a considerable boost for party funds. He expected two carols, the lantern light above his front door going on to indicate he had heard the first and was anticipating the second. He was Church. We were Chapel. But a pioneering ecumenical spirit laced mince pies and cocoa, and we knew he sent oranges and sweets to the Sunday School bunfight. A note in the collection box to cover all the coins drew murmurs of excitement, although the grown-ups as usual pretended not to notice. Ernie was almost moved to contrition for inviting shepherds to wash their socks by night.

There's something eerie about suggesting It Came Upon A Midnight Clear in pitch-blackness, and it was after such a rendition at one of the homes on the fringe of the parish that we three kings of close harmony decided to form a breakaway movement. Tubby and Ernie said they had only just recovered from nasty colds and ought to get home into the warm. I excused myself on grounds that I felt a sore throat coming on which could very well explain a distinct lack of enthusiasm for the last carol.

We headed for the other side of the village, strung out around the old aerodrome, appreciating the official warblers were most unlikely to get this far. Our aim was to add any financial bonus to the kitty for our Sunday School party. Our repertoire was limited without the sheets Harry had distributed and then recovered as we stole away into the night. Our musical dovetailing was highly erratic, three hesitant voices finding each other somewhere in the middle of a verse rather than at beginning or end. Frankly, it was more Donald Peers, Guy Mitchell and Frankie Laine than the Methodist Wandering Minstrels.

We collected two clear-offs, three you'll wake the kids up and four complaints about interfering with Radio Luxembourg reception before a widow, deaf and frail, eventually answered bangs on the door with a bemused smile and a crumpled copy of the Christian Herald. She insisted we take it, and then asked if we had seen the Tote Man. We promised to keep an eye out for his bike.

Disenchantment with the entire festive season was about to curtail our nocturnal endeavours when Tubby jabbed a finger in the general direction of Dikewood Farm. "Look, there's a light over there! Let's try one more Silent Night before we go." We moved towards the encouraging white blob in the blackness as a dog agitated at the end of a chain and the wind turned colder. A nothing-to-lose bravado accompanied our singing, and we managed two whole verses before I was volunteered to knock on the door. No reply. It was agreed to launch into Away In A Manger before Ernie tried his luck. The restless dog began to bark. Another light went on and a door opened somewhere behind us.

"Nice going, lads. Now we know Christmas is really on the way. How about a little number over here before you go? I'm sure you've done your bit for milk yields over there."

We had been carolling the cowshed. The farmer said our secret was safe with him as long as we could muster a serenade fit for a human audience. We had saved our best for last. As The Holly And The Ivy blossomed, and the cattle seemed to be lowing in time with the tune, the farmer slid a hand deep into his overall pocket and pulled out a shiny half-crown.

An old-fashioned Christmas card with
a timeless edge. Mistletoe, holly and a
gleaming face full of great expectations
make ideal decorations as we share
more joys with family and friends.

Great expectations

Despite the vast difference between what most of us wanted and what most of us got, the build-up to Christmas refused steadfastly to surrender any of its magic. True, we were not bombarded with televised temptations for weeks on end like today's blatantly-targeted youngsters, but we did allow ourselves a few more bouts of indulgence as the season of peace, goodwill and Tubby's double celebration drew closer.

Tubby got extra rations as his birthday fell on Christmas Day. We didn't know whether to envy or pity him. On one hand, he could ask for a really expensive main gift by combining both events. Then again, that was his lot for the year while we had another unwrapping session to come. As his best friend – and one of a family of ten children waiting for Santa to do understandably limited business – I liked it when he settled for the one big present. A real laced-up leather football or a proper cricket bat soaked with linseed oil meant our village sporting programme was safe for months to come. Tubby was a generous sort when it came to communal use of his prized possessions, although he brooked few arguments about who would bat first or go in goal on a hot day.

Excitement grew amid obvious village signs that Christmas was coming. Suddenly, the commonplace took on festive airs. Old worm-eaten pews in the chapel grinned through tinsel and holly as Sunday School party largesse needed to spread out. Our weekday school classroom transformed into a homely grotto as freshly-made trimmings trembled over the fireplace and paper lanterns danced above hot pipes at the back. The village shop windows turned bright and inviting as big tins of biscuits came under siege from soldiers, dolls, reindeer and crackers. Cotton-wool snow drifted everywhere along with little imaginations and great expectations. We huffed on the glass, rubbed it with our sleeves and pointed to favourite items lit up after school when before-tea darkness crept up so stealthily.

The domestic picture changed dramatically as well, not least with preparations for a fire in the front room for the first time since last Christmas. An extra sack of coal and a bigger pile of logs were just as pertinent pointers to the forthcoming festive season as a cockerel fattening at the bottom of the garden or the grocery delivery man's cardboard box overflowing.

Then came the trimming of the tree, a ritual designed to unleash a fresh torrent of anticipation. One of the few occasions when calls to join the fray did not meet with feeble excuses. Even the older, slightly more cynical members of the household readily lost themselves in a lengthy team effort to make it the brightest and busiest of beacons to family harmony and happiness over the best holiday of the year.

Mother started to stockpile little chocolate decorations at the end of November, a secret horde on top of the wardrobe drawing gasps of admiration when she presented them for inspection alongside new baubles, old stars and candle-holders borrowed from a woman up the road who was experimenting with them new-fangled electric lights. It took steady hands and the best part of an evening to reach that crowning moment when the angel (of Norfolk Methodist stock with a halo on the sosh) looked down upon a kaleidoscope of Christmas crafting and decreed that it was good.

"Oh, nearly forgot," said Mother, bustling towards the darkest corner of the pantry. She returned with six pink sugar mice, plump and beady-eyed, ready to dangle bravely from any unclaimed branch. And thereby hangs a tale of temptation equalled only by well-chronicled events in the Garden of Eden. Another time. Another tree. Another trial. But the same old serpent of seduction. My passion for sugar mice turned the next two weeks into a torture trail, especially when I lingered and lusted on my way past the tree towards the old rickety stairs to bed. I knew all my dreams would involve snipping, snaffling, hiding and trying to talk with a mouth crammed full of pink candy.

The joy and spirit of Christmas is captured perfectly in the faces of these children as they celebrate the age-old story at a Norfolk nativity.

A brazen voice tried to convince me that one tiny mouse could hardly be missed. Who had been counting amid all that trimming excitement? Another siren suggested a big family meant too many suspects for serious grilling at a time of rich benevolence. A furtive whisper campaign started against all cats in the neighbourhood, particularly those who could creep in unnoticed and spirit away a tasty morsel without parting a loaded tree from its papered pot. Now I was clutching at claws and felt ashamed to even contemplate blaming dumb animals after moving scenes in the school nativity play.

I was seriously tempted to compromise at least one brother and two sisters who had split on me over missing bananas in July, watered-down ginger beer in August and a late-night raid on Dad's Woodbine packet before we went back to school in September.

In the end, true Christmas spirit prevailed and six pink sugar mice survived – to be cut down and wrapped up as contributions to pass-the-parcel fun at the village hall party. I was just too old to join in, but mustered sincere smiles for the winners.

As far as I could remember, they were in for a treat.

We Three Sages

Some of the threads holding this seasonal narrative together may have more to do with the gossamer of imagination than the binder-twine of reality. Truth is, I got carried away on a tide of sheer romance as soon as the first trimmings and paper lanterns began dancing above our desks.

While Christmas preparations reached a crescendo in the village school classroom, I often found it impossible to distinguish fact from fantasy. On at least two occasions in the early 1950s, when post-war austerity still put a brake on many festive ambitions, I convinced myself that the cockerel we were fattening up for the family dinner on the big day would fly the roost hours before execution to deliver itself willingly to a frail old couple desperately in need of a square meal. Reckon it was my way of recognising the true message of Christmas – much more blessed to give than to receive – or, perhaps, an acknowledgement of growing fondness for the strutting, preening, belligerent creature marking his domain beyond the lilac bushes.

In any event, I swallowed all misgivings and tucked in with the rest once it had been transformed into a golden gift for the carving knife. Surely no-one went hungry at this time of peace, goodwill and overworked ovens. Quiet beyond the lilac bushes could not give way to any kind of guilt as soon as the washing-up was done…

The school nativity play inspired its own fanciful notions before traditional virtues bounded out from the wings. I longed for the biggest nuisances to be cast as angels, the most academically-challenged to march on as the Three Wise Men and a couple who couldn't stand the sight of each other to be drawn together as Mary and Joseph. Such clear incentives, to throw off the threadbare garments of predictability and cheap reputation, and to don rich robes from the wardrobe of fresh direction and brand new persona. The challenge was never collared. I was way ahead of my time as an educational psychologist.

"Horses for courses," meant gold, frankincense and myrrh for Tubby, Ernie and me. I can't remember who first suggested it, but the idea of replacing pretend camels with real bicycles as means of transport to the stable was voted down by producer, director, stage manager and the rest of the cast as a potential hazard too far. The follow-up suggestion of three boys on one machine – sort of biblical precursors of The Goodies – met with a similarly emphatic "Just go away and learn your lines".

The odd halo got buckled or broken during rehearsals when shepherds high on creative juices tried a spot of pigtail-pulling among the angels. The odd sheep went missing as cherubic smiles surrendered to the cause of grim retribution. We three sages, clearly in a different class when it came to dramatic interpretation and experience of the big-time, were simply trusted to live up to the old maxim that it would all come right on the afternoon.

Ernie threatened to turn his gift into 'Frankenstein' because he'd heard someone say it in the shop and all the customers laughed. We told him it had been done before, and it wasn't truly in keeping with the Christmas story. Tubby thought Wise Men in hobnailed boots would cause a big stir and let the audience know we were on our way. While I liked the prospect of a grand entry, this seemed unnecessarily extravagant and might frighten little ones near the front. We settled for plimsolls and the magnetism of our cloaked personalities.

It did go quite well on the afternoon when proud relatives and important folk of the village, like the parson, parish council chairman and a sprinkling of school governors, smiled benevolently, mimed softly and applauded enthusiastically.

Only blot on this Bethlehem landscape (apart from a damp patch near the back where an anxious angel misinterpreted references to a pool of light) arrived with our take-a-bow finale. Simmering hostilities between shepherds and the heavenly host threatened to boil over when the former, predominantly boys, barged the angels, mostly girls, out of the road as they beamed to the front. Part of a curtain was torn. A clear case of too many crooks spoiling the cloth.

We stooped to conquer, our bows beautifully synchronised, our collective wisdom earning knowing nods from the elders of the village. We appreciated how this potent image would stand us in excellent stead on carol-singing rounds coming up.

"Ah, the Three Wise Men reversing roles, seeking gifts from us for their collecting boxes. Such sound lads. Audrey, fetch my wallet and large slices of that fruit cake you made this afternoon."

We licked our lips, milked the applause and wondered how on earth they would cope next year when we had left the stage to follow our stars to bigger schools and small parts as sword carriers.

Young angels, shepherds, wise men, Mary and Joseph… they come together in countless communities to tell the most wonderful story of all at Christmastime.

Going home

Going home is an act of faith in the past
A remembrance service with only hymns that you know
A demand to recognise the changeless before it goes
Glorious delusion that hurts no-one and
smiles on all who want it

Going home is an open path out of the present
A revivalist tent on the green for your jaded senses
An offer to recognise the changeable while it lasts
Serious confusion to hurt someone
who smiles at all who knows it

Going home is not the same as going back
It is giving more or less than you used to and
only you know if that's enough to keep interest alive
Or a glorious illusion to force a smile out of all who see it.

Keith Skipper
(on going home to Beeston, 1991)